THE
LITTLE
HISTORY

OF

KENT

THE
LITTLE
HISTORY
OF
KENT

SUSAN HIBBERD

First published 2019
Reprinted 2021, 2023

The History Press
97 St George's Place,
Cheltenham, Gloucestershire, GL50 3QB
www.thehistorypress.co.uk

British Library Cataloguing in Publication Data.
A catalogue record for this book is available from the British Library.

ISBN 978 0 7509 9006 6

Typesetting and origination by The History Press
Printed by TJ Books Limited, Padstow, Cornwall

CONTENTS

INTRODUCTION

For the vast majority of visitors to the United Kingdom, Kent is the first place they see, as it was for the hunter-gatherers who travelled from Africa. The people of Kent have not only lived under the rule of Romans, Saxons and Normans – they have seen these invaders come and go from their very shores, and resisted many more. Spanish, Dutch and German invaders have been repelled, while refugees from persecution in France, Germany, Belgium and the Netherlands have been welcomed and offered sanctuary.

The county is wrapped in a 350-mile coastline, which offers a range of habitats and landscapes. Marshes and wetlands, shingle and beaches, woodlands, chalk uplands, wide fertile plains, rolling hills and valleys are all part of the Kentish landscape, along with 250 miles of inland waterways. The county is much like a human palm, criss-crossed with pathways; the chalky ridge of the North Downs shows on a map as the love line and the Greensand Way describes the lifeline. The industrial areas in the north are echoed in the development at Dungeness.

This is the story of a front-line county, with tales of invasion, rebellion, resistance and a surprising number of elephants. Enjoy the journey and come and visit us soon.

The logo of Fremlin's brewery

1

IN THE BEGINNING

The first Kentish family walked into our landscape during the Palaeolithic period, a time that most of us would call the Stone Age. The dinosaurs were long gone, although the skeleton of an iguanodon lay hidden in the Maidstone area, and the land was newly released from the glaciers of the Ice Age.

MONKEYS AND ELEPHANTS

The landscape this family inhabited was open tundra, which had been scoured by repeated cooling and warming of the climate from the Ice Age to tropical conditions that were home to animals like elephants and monkeys. They followed their prey as it migrated, hunting for food and collecting roots and berries from the plants around them. Their main concern would have been finding a reliable supply of fresh water, and archaeological finds show that they followed the meanderings of the rivers, making temporary camps when they needed to rest or to butcher a kill. Any Kentish gardener knows that flint is abundant within the chalky soil of the Downs, and Kentish man worked with the materials around him, crafting the stone tools that identify this period.

Although the Stone Age, including the Palaeolithic and Mesolithic eras, lasted almost 700,000 years, little changed in Kent throughout this time. Several human species came to the county, waiting as the sea levels rose and fell, so they could cross from the continent while the area presently occupied by the English Channel was dry. They shared their world with woolly mammoth and woolly rhino. Several sites along the North Kent coast continue to throw up mammoth teeth and the bones of animals that were killed by man, although there is no evidence that they cooked the meat before eating it. Despite the concentration of finds in areas like Oldbury Hill, it is probable that only 250 or so Stone Age people lived in Kent.

One particularly spectacular Stone Age site has been identified near Tunbridge Wells at the site we call High Rocks. Sandstone cliffs up to 80ft tall in places provide a venue for leisure today, but would once have offered valuable protection from predators. The site has been identified as a National Monument.

Only two skulls from this period have ever been found in Britain, and the earliest is that of a Kentish man, who would have stood about 3ft high. He died in the area around Swanscombe, close to the Bluewater Shopping Centre, near flint tools and animal bones – the remains of a Stone Age dinner. Excavations at Swanscombe also revealed the teasing glimpse of a straight-tusked elephant, and archaeologists were thrilled to find an almost complete skeleton during the building of Ebbsfleet International Station in 2004, including several piles of discarded flint tools, used for butchering the animal and thrown to one side as they blunted. Evidence of Stone Age man is also found at Fordwich, near Canterbury, a town which features much in the ongoing history of

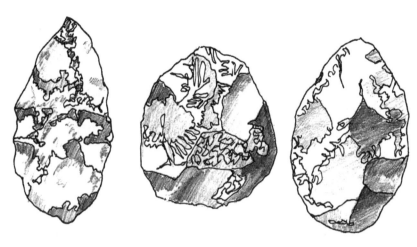

Flint tools of the kind often found in Kent

Kent. Although there are hundreds of sites across the county with evidence of Palaeolithic man, the most important of these are in the Cuxton and Sturry areas. Special mention should also be made of the fabulous Neanderthal hand axe or coupe found near Maidstone, which dates to about 60,000 BC.

There is some academic disagreement about whether Neanderthals eradicated the families they found living in Britain, intermarried, or just lived alongside them. The Neanderthals were shorter than modern humans, standing between 5ft and 5ft 6in high, were heavier set and significantly more muscular. However, they were a long way from the shambling half-ape stereotypes seen on film and TV, and would not look out of place if seen in a modern High Street.

HOMO SAPIENS ARRIVES

Soon after this, the face of the Kentish family changed, as *Homo sapiens* made an appearance. These were even more like a modern human, and they gradually took the land from the Neanderthals, either by force or, more likely, through gradual interbreeding. They were culturally more sophisticated, using finer bone tools and creating cave paintings to represent themselves and their lifestyle.

As our Kentish family settled into a routine, they became skilled at creating the flint tools they needed, making a variety of different styles for cutting, chopping or fine slicing; examples have been found near Finglesham and Lenham. The landscape around them had also developed, becoming heavily wooded. This woodland would have been home to horses, deer, sabretoothed cats and hyenas, many much smaller than we know today, and it provided the materials needed to fuel their fires. In 1839, fossils of an animal the size of a spaniel were found near Herne Bay which were later proven to be the remains of the earliest-known horse.

By 5,000 BC there were an estimated 6,000 people living in England, most of whom lived in Kent. Shortly after this the causeway from the continent flooded for the last time. Britain became an island and our Kentish family, with their friends and relatives, were on their own.

THE NEW STONE AGE

The New Stone Age, or Neolithic period, covered just over 1,000 years, from 4,000 BC onwards. The Kentish family no longer lived a nomadic lifestyle, but had moved into a village set on the chalk uplands, where the woods grew less thickly and danger could be anticipated. Their house was a wooden log cabin, and was set up near pens for the sheep, pigs, goats and cattle of the village. Although some of the men went out hunting for meat, many also sowed crops to supplement their foraging, which provided a more stable way of life. The discovery of ancient quern stones shows that the family was grinding grain and possibly baking simple flatbreads as well as using grain to make pottage or frumenty, a thick porridge flavoured with berries and herbs.

When the crops became less productive, due to depletion of the nutrients in the soil, the villagers simply moved on, clearing woodland at their new site if they needed to.

This more settled lifestyle gave the family time to think and reflect on the nature of life. They wore jewellery, made pottery and buried their dead in communal tombs called long barrows. One such barrow, or dolmen tomb, is located on a hillside near Aylesford, its entrance guarded by stoneworks which have been named Kit's Coty House, a group of stones 8ft high supporting a 10-ton capstone. Little Kit's Coty House is less than a mile away but is known as the Countless Stones as it is no longer standing. Another Kentish family group lived near Chilham and created the long barrow we call Juliberrie's Grave.

An even more spectacular site is that of the Coldrum Long Barrow found near the village of Trottiscliffe (pronounced 'Trossley'), a stone construction celebrated as one of the Medway Megaliths which appear on either side of the Medway river, all built of local sarsen stone. When the site was excavated, the remains of twenty-two people were discovered, along with the bones of several animals. These contrast with the earthen barrows of the Stour Valley in the more eastern parts of the county, which were constructed where stone was unavailable, and of which little remains.

The Kentish clan was always busy, but during this period the communities found time to create at least four causewayed enclosures, two at Eastchurch on the Isle of Sheppey, and two near Ramsgate, at Chalk Hill and Pegwell Bay. These were regular, usually oval, shapes, outlined with one or more rows of banks and ditches, used for special gatherings of many local tribes.

Later, as their tool-making improved, they created henges and wooden circles, such as the one at Ringlemere, near Sandwich The Ringlemere henge consisted of a circular hill about 40yd wide surrounded by a 15ft ditch and may have been used for communal celebrations. As recently as 2014, another Neolithic henge consisting of two concentric ring ditches almost 100ft across was found near Iwade when developers dug the foundations for a housing estate.

The settled lifestyle of the Kentish family was soon to be upended, however, as a new wave of immigrants arrived from the continent. The Bronze Age was approaching.

THE BRONZE AGE

A little later than 2,000 BC, the Beaker People arrived in Britain from Holland and Germany, which swelled the population of England to about 300,000. They were followed by the Celts, who brought with them a new culture, including the knowledge of how to melt copper and tin together to make bronze, a much harder metal than either of its constituent parts. This changed the lives of the indigenous population, and enriched it. One of the remarkable mysteries about this period is that Kent has no tin. The tin for their bronze must have been brought from the West Country, showing that there was already trade throughout Britain even at this early stage.

It is commonly acknowledged that trade had been carried out between Britain and the continent for hundreds of years. One of the most spectacular pieces of evidence is the Bronze Age boat discovered in 1992 which has found a home in Dover Museum. The boat was never fully excavated from the mud surrounding it, for fear of further deterioration, but it is certainly the oldest seagoing vessel ever found. The boat, which would have made several journeys across the English Channel, was constructed from oak planks, held together with wooden wedges and thin, flexible yew branches. The boat was able to carry sixteen crew and up to 3 tonnes of cargo.

The spectacular Margate Shell Grotto, discovered by the Victorians in 1835, is as yet undated, but is generally considered to be from the Bronze Age; the walls and ceiling of both the cave and the access tunnels are covered with intricate shell mosaics in a variety of patterns. Most of the shells occur locally, but the flat winkle, which is used as an infill between the major motifs, can only be found near Southampton. It is tempting to think that Kentish man traded along the south coast using a boat similar to that found at Dover.

People on the continental side of the Channel were very similar to those in Kent, wearing skins, farming, making pottery, harvesting berries and shellfish, and living in round wooden houses, and they may have traded precious stones, gold or particularly fine examples of pottery or jewellery across the Channel. In 1974, divers found an underwater hoard of Bronze Age tools and weapons in Langdon Bay that are considered to be part of a trading agreement between people in Kent and those living in modern-day France. Over 100 objects were recovered, and it is thought that they were being brought to Britain to be smelted down and repurposed.

Once on land, those visitors, or immigrants, wishing to travel further inland followed a route called the causeway which ran from Folkestone to Wye and on into Farnham, possibly travelling even further to the west, as we know the people of Kent traded with those in the West Country for materials that were unavailable locally.

At the beginning of the period, people who died were usually interred in long barrows or round barrows, with or without grave goods. These were often grouped together, as seen at Monkton in Thanet. The henge that had been built at Ringlemere was enhanced with the addition of a long barrow, and in 2001, a metal detectorist unearthed a gold cup of international significance, traded from Ireland. However, by the end of the period, burial sites such as this were no longer used. There is a small cemetery at Bridge, near Canterbury, which was used for a short while, but eventually formal burial rites ceased or became such that they left no trace.

In 2013 the remains of another Bronze Age henge was discovered at Sonora Fields near Sittingbourne, which revealed the remains of pottery, tools, a human urn burial and a human skeleton.

The Kentish family had ambition, and improved their farming skills, extending their enclosures and rearing more livestock; there is certainly evidence of Neolithic ploughing at Folkestone, where furrows can be seen. The influence of the Celtic language exists in place names such as Sarre, Chevening and Lympne, and by the end of the Neolithic period, the family had learnt the metalworking skills of the Celtic migrants and were smelting bronze and moulding the items they needed using wet sand. They were weaving, making pots, harvesting salt from the sea on the Hadlow Marshes, near Romney, or at the aptly named Seasalter and devising a range of weaponry. Bronze swords have been discovered at Chatham and Aylesford, alongside other weapons and agricultural tools at Minster, Marden and Birchington.

Perhaps the Kentish people saw the future on the horizon, because before long those weapons were needed in the defence of their home.

THE IRON AGE

As the Roman Empire spread across the continent, tribes were displaced and fled. The Franks and the Visigoths, among others, crossed into Britain. Our Kentish family had already felt the impact of the Celtic influx and in 100 BC helped to build forts at places like Bigbury, Keston, Capel and Oldbury. The one at Oldbury was the largest and covered over 150 acres of land. The ramparts and ditches of another fort, at Dover, provided the base for the medieval castle that was later built on the same spot. The port was already an important entrance to the country and Dover is still known as the 'Gateway to England'. These forts were large defended earthworks within which were barns, workshops and housing.

As it turned out, these tribes were again assimilated into the Kentish culture, and they brought with them many skills, such as the use of iron instead of bronze. Iron was no harder than bronze, but was much cheaper to produce and lighter to carry. After an early start near Herne Bay, the centre of iron production in Kent developed in the village of Bedgebury, which was rich in local ironstone and so quickly expanded. The blood of the Kentish family was now mixed with that of their continental cousins.

At the end of the period Britain became home to the Belgae people from northern France, who brought with them ploughs and pottery wheels. They maintained contact with their fellow countrymen and traded corn, iron and slaves for pottery, amber and gold.

Political centres were created, and in 20 BC Canterbury became the Iron Age capital of Britain. Examples of local coinage have been found that were minted at Canterbury, but it is not thought that the tokens were used as we use money today; they were possibly exchanged at the time a contract was agreed as a sign of good faith. Kent worked as a kingdom divided into tribes under various leaders, with the Belgic tribe being most prevalent to the east of the River Medway and the Wealden people to the west. The language of the Belgic tribe was very similar to that of the inhabitants of Gaul, across the Channel, and this enabled trade deals to be carried out quickly and easily.

The Kentish family had moved to a larger village, possibly enclosed with a ditch or even a row of fencing. Their round wooden house was much warmer as it was made of wattle and daub, a lattice of wooden struts infilled with a mixture of mud, straw and manure, and a thatched roof to keep it cosy. Archaeological evidence of such housing has been found at Farningham and Ashford. Some of the men sowed crops, some tended the animals, and some enjoyed hunting, bringing back wild boar and other game from the surrounding woodlands. Confirmation of their hunting skills is found at Farningham Hill, where deer bones have been excavated. The deer had been killed with iron daggers and butchered with iron knives, after which their skins would have been processed with an array of tools, including scrapers and awls. Our family dressed in woven clothing, which suggests they kept sheep alongside their horses, oxen and dogs.

It was only sixty years after this that the lives of the Kentish family were again changed forever, and the echoes of this change are with us still, for it was the coming of the Romans.

The White Cliffs of Dover

2

THE ROMANS

⇥ 55 BC–AD 410 ⇤

VENI, VEDI, VICI

The people of Kent had worked to improve the land and to create settlements, and they had negotiated trade agreements with tribes on the continent for their excess goods. News of this land of plenty with its rich agricultural soil and generous mineral deposits reached Rome and in 55 BC Julius Caesar attempted to invade.

Seeing the towering white cliffs at Dover, Caesar travelled further around the coast to Walmer, where he landed his troops. The invasion was short-lived, as a storm damaged the Roman fleet and Caesar decided to fall back to Gaul before further damage occurred. He tried again the next year, bringing 600 ships, 17,000 soldiers and 2,000 cavalry with him. He landed at Deal and fought his way to London. Weakened by the Belgic tribes who had taken over Bigbury fort, he returned home two months later; although he had managed to negotiate an annual tribute from the Britons and established trade links, Britain remained largely unconquered. Our Kentish family heard tell of an invading army, but many of them considered it to be a myth; their daily lives were unchanged by the political agreements made outside their immediate experience.

Even at this early date, Kent already had its name, as Julius Caesar recorded the area as Cantium, home of the Cantii people.

INVADERS WITH ELEPHANTS

In AD 43 the family were amazed to see Roman galleons once more sailing along the eastern coast and landing 50,000 men at Richborough, near Sandwich. Some reports say that they brought one or more elephants with them, which would indeed have astounded and terrified the Kentish folk. The coastline has changed through time, and today Richborough is inland, but it was at that time on a convenient land promontory in the sheltered Wantsum Channel which divided the Isle of Thanet from the mainland. Despite fierce resistance, including an unprecedented two-day battle at Medway, the Romans triumphed and Plautius became the ruler of Kent.

The Romans were keen to update their new territory and immediately built a road through Canterbury to London, along with many fortifications, starting with a huge fort at Richborough (Rutupiae) which became their main port. They also used Dover (Dubris) and Reculver (Regulbium), which was manned by soldiers from western Germany.

In about AD 50 they built two lighthouses, one on either side of Dover's river, the Dour. Only the eastern one survives, as the Pharos Roman lighthouse. The lighthouse was originally six floors high, and it is estimated that it stood 80ft tall when it was first built, with a beacon lit at the top during the night. Today it still stands 60ft high, thanks to medieval restoration work. The fort they built at Reculver was situated on the Thames and guarded the entrance to the Wantsum Channel, which at that time was over 2 miles wide. The channel gradually silted up, eventually filling in completely during a series of storms in the Tudor period, and its position is now identified by a flat expanse of marshy farmland labelled with a small road sign. The name of the nearby village St Nicholas-at-Wade gives an indication that it grew up when it was possible to ford the shallow water at the narrowest section.

Reculver Towers as they look today

DAILY LIFE

Our Kentish family kept their heads down and life in their tiny village was pretty much unaffected, except for the new opportunities for trade with the Romans, who needed grain, meat, leather, wool, beer, etc. as well as made goods. For relatives who lived in the towns, though, the pace of life changed dramatically. The Roman invaders built sprawling villas, markets and temples with central heating and flowing water. Villas were concentrated around the Medway and Darent valleys as it was easier to transport building materials along rivers than along the as-yet-unfinished roads. The presence of wharf facilities at Eccles, on the Medway, shows that the sites were chosen to enable the easy delivery of goods during the period of occupation and possibly to hasten the export of manufactured items. Workshops and stores at the Eccles site especially seem to support the manufacture of pottery, which would have been sent to other parts of the Roman Empire within Britain and maybe even further afield. The Kentish family enjoyed oysters, cockles and whelks as part of their diet, which were harvested at Whitstable and other north-coast villages.

The administrative centres of Canterbury and Rochester expanded quickly and work was available both within the Roman community and outside. It is possible to get a glimpse of Roman life at the Lullingstone Roman Villa, where you can see the heated bath-house, the mosaics and prints of the wall paintings. The villa had separate rooms for Christian and pagan worship. Nearly a hundred villas have been found in Kent, the best examples being at Darenth, Wingham and Folkestone as well as at Lullingstone. The site at Darenth, on the River Darent, is particularly important as the site had been in constant use since the Mesolithic period, through the Roman occupation and into Anglo-Saxon times.

Canterbury became an important town, and was protected by city walls made of flint, measuring 30ft high and 6ft wide, pierced with six gateways and protected by twenty-one watchtowers. Within the walls were a group of four burial mounds, created soon after the Romans arrived, known until the eighteenth century as the Dungeon or Don Jon, and now housed within the Dane John Gardens. The town boasted a market square, a public bath-house and an open-air theatre.

One building our Kentish family would certainly not have visited was the town house in central Canterbury, which had a superb floor mosaic, now protected by the Canterbury Roman Museum; nor would they have seen the Roman hotel built for travellers at Dover, the painted walls of which can be viewed at the Roman Painted House Museum which has been built around it. These had been constructed for the very richest Romans who would have had nothing to do with the lowly locals.

Falling somewhere between the poorer housing of our Kentish family and the opulent Roman villas were timber-built towns such as that found at Westhawk Farm, Ashford, which is much like a small village of today with a shrine, a cemetery, housing and a smithy. Roman temples were dotted throughout the county, some more elaborate than others; at Springhead, archaeologists have found the remains of several temples around the one natural spring, and the Kentish family would have been welcomed at these if they wished to worship the Roman gods. One of the temples was situated near the church of St Mary's at Stone-in-Oxney where part of an altar stone gives its name to the village, and the remains of another can be seen at Boxted.

The Kentish family was familiar with the purely Kentish concept of the Hooden Horse, the origins of which have been all but lost. In AD 690, after the Romans had left, Theodore, Archbishop of Canterbury condemned the practice of donning animal skins for pagan rites, which shows that the practice was already a long-standing local custom. Nowadays, the Hooden Horse is for the most part restricted to outings at Christmas when it accompanies carol singers collecting for charity or autumnal hop festivities such as the annual Hop Hoodening at Canterbury Cathedral.

Of course, the Romans felt the need to defend themselves, so they extended the fort at Richborough and built more forts at key sites like Reculver. These were used as bases for their ships as well as sentry points to repel attack. Even Richborough was remodelled, and in about AD 90 the Romans built a massive arch, reported to be over 82ft high, to mark the entrance to the overseas territory which they called Britannia. This was clad in marble and would have been visible to ships well before they landed on British soil. Visitors can easily make out the foundations of this arch at the site and see the remains of the town, including its amphitheatre.

ROMAN ROADS

As the Romans settled in, they built more roads, the most famous of which is Watling Street, which runs from Richborough into Canterbury (Durovernum), and on to Rochester (Durobrivae) before crossing the Thames in London and eventually making its way to Chester, Wales and then on to Holyhead, where they could cross into Ireland. Kent's chalky landscape was ideal for road building, as its free-draining nature kept the roads dry, unlike highways built on clay soil. Other Roman roads radiate from Canterbury to link with Dover, Lympne (Portus Lemanis), Reculver and Benenden, and run from Dover up to Richborough and also across to Maidstone. The iron trade was strong in the area, and a main road went through the Weald linking the Medway with Sussex.

Roman roads were wide, high and paved, unlike anything ever seen in Britain before. They were constructed so that rainwater ran off into the gutters alongside, thus keeping the surface dry, and this meant they could be as much as 10m wide. A rare paved ford can be seen at Iden, near Benenden, measuring almost 12ft wide. Our Kentish family may have snuck out when the day ended to look at the work being done and to see how their wooden causeways were being replaced by modern technological design.

Many of the vineyards that dot the Kentish countryside were started by the Romans. The Domesday survey records sites at Chart Sutton, Chislet and Leeds, and although by the time of Henry VIII 139 vineyards were in operation, the practice of cultivating vines was never seriously revised until the 1970s. Today, Kent boasts some of the largest vineyards in the country, with that at Lamberhurst being perhaps the largest.

The Romans stayed for almost 400 years, and we still feel the impact of their occupation in the way our towns are laid out, the road system and particularly the advances in plumbing and sanitation. The people of Kent improved their agricultural systems in order to supply the Roman settlements with food, adopted the Julian calendar and started to use the Latin language, which has persisted in the disciplines of law and science. Our family may not have liked the amount of bureaucracy entailed in even the most mundane of transactions, but they would certainly have appreciated the new foods that were imported and the advances in trading standards.

However, by AD 410 the well-oiled administrative machine which ran the Roman Empire had broken down, the troops were recalled and the Kentish family was surprised to find that their home was no longer occupied by a foreign nation. Britons maintained trade links with the continent, sending out cattle, corn and precious metals, and importing wine, oil and pottery. The villas remained, the roads remained, even some of the Romans remained, but Kent was once more in control of its own destiny.

The Kentish Hooden Horse can still be seen in folk celebrations around the county

3

THE ANGLES, SAXONS AND JUTES

⊰ 410–1065 ⊱

The Kentish families living in the network of tiny villages across the county will have felt the leaving of the Romans much less than those in the town, where the whole infrastructure of day-to-day life gradually unravelled. The town of Canterbury seems to have been almost completely abandoned during this period, with the inhabitants maybe moving to London to cling to the lifestyle they had come to enjoy.

Once the Romans had gone, political rumblings started throughout Britain as tribal chiefs began to gather armies and fight against each other, although they eventually came together under Vortigern, the High King. To counter the threat of invasion from the Picts and the Scots, Bede tells us that Vortigern asked the Angles, Saxons and Jutes from northern Germany and Denmark to help. They came in AD 446, led by Hengist and Horsa, and landed near Richborough at Pegwell Bay, travelling across the sea in three longships;

the broad bay offered an easy landing spot with its shallow, sheltered waters. A replica longship, the *Hugin*, can be seen beside the main road at Pegwell Bay, commemorating the event. The ship was rowed here in 1949 by modern-day Danes, who observed authentic Viking conditions on-board apart from the one instrument they took with them, a sextant.

The mercenaries, seeing the disarray within Britain, fought their way across Kent and southern England, battling at Aylesford, Crayford and Ebbsfleet, taking control as they went. Eventually, they divided Britain between them. The Saxons took over Sussex, Wessex and Essex, the Angles took East Anglia, Mercia and Northumbria, and the Jutes (led by the Angles Hengist and Horsa) stayed in Kent, adopting the white horse as their symbol. The seven kingdoms are recognised as the Anglo-Saxon Heptarchy and remained for almost 500 years; the name England may have developed from the phrase Angle-Land. Surprisingly, recent genetic studies have shown that there was very little intermarriage between the Anglo-Saxons and the Celtic Britons, and that the Celts were not pushed out of the area completely, as was previously thought. Our Kentish family may not have liked their Jutish rulers, but they managed to co-exist quite amicably.

DIVIDED KENT

The Jutes comprised several tribes and over time our Kentish family did became part-Celtic and part-Jute. Two main administrative areas grew up at Eastry (Eastorege) and Sturry (Storigao), and were used while Canterbury (Cantwarabyrig) was being rebuilt. Some of the Saxon mercenaries stayed in Kent, settling the western villages, and it might be this Jute/Saxon split which gave rise to the differentiation between Men of Kent in the east and Kentish Men in the west. Differences in burial customs between east and west Kent also point to this as a time of division. A rare hlaew burial mound in Juniper Wood near Wye is an example of the Saxon custom of burying high-status individuals. Further evidence of a divided Kent comes from the suggestion in some documents of the time that there were in fact two Kings of Kent, and also from the irrefutable fact that there are two cathedral cities.

Although many families fled to the west of Britain, our Kentish family carried on life as normal, living a mainly agricultural lifestyle, while fighting took place between the professional soldiers. The language they spoke on a daily basis changed to incorporate the more Germanic terminology of the Jutes, and they were glad that they no longer had to remember the Latin insisted on by the Romans for administration or trade. The two languages had a common Belgic root, so they may have understood each other reasonably well, and the languages merged and eventually evolved into what we know as Old English. Place names which originate from the Jutish language are those ending in –inge, -ynge or -linge, such as Beltinge and Lyminge.

DAILY LIFE

For the Kentish family, life carried on almost unchanged, although there was less wealth in the county. They had kept away from the Romans as much as possible, trading with them only when necessary, and mostly stayed on their farm, building up their smallholding. They wore the linen tunics of the previous period, short for the men and long for the women, with belts and brooches to keep them in place. Their diet was based on daily stews using the vegetables and grains they grew, with parsnips as a base for many dishes as the potato had not yet been introduced. They kept their wooden single-roomed home with a thatched roof, perhaps living on the north Kent coast at Merston, where the remains of a stockade village from this period have been found.

The Jutes had a slightly different way of ruling than the Angles and Saxons. The county was divided into at least seven districts called lathes, from the Jutish word for an administrative unit: Aylesford, Milton, Sutton, Borough, Eastry, Lympne and Wye. However, this information is taken from the Domesday Book and enumerators may have omitted some smaller lathes. Lathes, which were further divided into areas named hundreds, and then further into parishes, became the basis for the administrative districts which remain in place today.

One notable difference in law was the practice of gavelkind, or partible inheritance, under which many people could inherit the wealth of the deceased, and which led to the division of the land into smaller and smaller units. This contrasted with the rule of primogeniture which covered the rest of Britain, where only the eldest inherited. Partly due to this law, Kent was never subject to the open field system of agriculture which predominated in other parts of the country, where common land is farmed in rotation by different villagers. In Kent, each man jealously guarded his own land, passing it from father to son. The gavelkind laws also allowed a wife to inherit half her husband's estate on his death, whereas in other parts of the country it could be as low as one third. The innocent relatives of those accused of criminal activity also benefited; in other parts of Britain a felon's lands were forfeit to the king, but in Kent they were passed to his (or her) descendants. Gavelkind was not rescinded until 1925.

In their religious life, the people of Kent may have persisted in their worship of local gods or the Roman gods Jupiter, Mars and Mercury, or they may have moved towards gods from the religions of Egypt or Syria, perhaps continuing to attend the Roman temples that dotted the countryside. Christianity did not arrive in Britain for another 150 years.

Hengist, Horsa and their descendants ruled Kent for the next 100 years, and were followed by Ethelbert, who became the first Christian king in Britain, and encouraged his subjects to change to the new religion. The church of St Martin's in Canterbury was built during the Roman occupation, before the arrival of St Augustine, and it has been in continuous use as a place of worship ever since. Along with Canterbury Cathedral and St Augustine's Abbey in Canterbury, it is a World Heritage Site.

THE COMING OF CHRISTIANITY

Invited by King Ethelbert and Queen Bertha, St Augustine arrived in Kent in AD 597, with forty followers. He landed at Pegwell Bay, as had Hengist and Horsa before him, and the place where he stopped and said his first mass on British soil is marked by a stone cross, just to the west of Cliffs End. After meeting King Ethelbert at

Richborough he was granted land in Canterbury, where he took over a disused Roman church and made it the centre of Christianity in Britain. Sadly, the cathedral he built was destroyed by fire in 1067, although it is possible that some of the foundations survive under the present building. Rochester Cathedral was founded in AD 604 by Bishop Justus, and the present building was completed in 1080.

St Martin's Church, Canterbury

The Roman Catholic religion flourished and our Kentish family may have visited Minster Abbey, in Ramsgate, or one of the new cathedrals at Rochester or Canterbury; Kent was the only kingdom divided into two sees with archbishops at both Rochester and Canterbury. Not all families took to the new religion immediately, and many kept up their old ways of worship for many hundreds of years. The ruins of the Anglo-Saxon chapel at Stone-next-Faversham are a unique example of the way Anglo-Saxon builders re-used materials, as the building incorporates parts of a Romano-British pagan mausoleum.

The kings of Kent changed regularly, but the county stayed under the control of a High King or Ruler of Britain as a whole – at one time Kent came under the rule of Mercia. The area became known as Cantia in around AD 730 and in AD 825 Kent became part of Wessex, under King Alfred the Great. Ten years later the name Cent was in general use.

Some of the Roman infrastructure, particularly the roads, did not fall into disuse, although travel by sea and river was in some cases a better option as the countryside was once again becoming covered in woodland. At the time the Romans came, much of the Weald was covered in forest, too dangerous to cross, and many village names such as Lamberhurst, Hawkhurst and Goudhurst support this, as 'hurst' was the word for a forest or wood.

Trade and manufacture had recovered from the decline which followed the end of the Roman Empire, and stone buildings, primarily churches, started to appear in the landscape. Dover, Canterbury and Rochester were still the three main towns and they continued to grow in importance. Canterbury and Rochester even had their own mints, and although ships sailed up the river to Appledore and Smallhythe, the reclamation of the land currently so valuable for sheep farming had begun.

The Kentish scilling or sceatt was worth more than shillings in other parts of the country

OUR OWN CURRENCY

It was at this time that an early type of currency came into general use, although the Kentish shilling differed from that used in other parts of the country – even from that of Wessex. The Kentish coins were sceatts and scillings, roughly equivalent to pennies and shillings. This Kentish shilling was the weight of a Roman ounce, whereas shillings in other parts of the country could be worth as little as a third of this.

VIKING ATTACKS

Kent was lucky enough to have suffered less from the early Viking raids which so beleaguered northern counties. The Vikings, or Norsemen, came from Scandinavia and conquered much of England, Europe, Iceland and even parts of what is now the United States of America. The first raid was on Sheppey in AD 835, and seven years later the major towns of Rochester and Canterbury were targeted. Luckily for Kent, Alfred the Great negotiated the Treaty of Wedmore in AD 878 and the Norsemen mostly settled in northern and central Britain, which left the kings of Wessex and Mercia to govern the south. For this reason, Kent was never subject to the Danish law, or Danelaw, that plagued much of the country.

Further attacks followed, and in AD 892 a different Viking group attacked, coming from part of the Norse empire in France; 250 ships sailed along the south coast of Kent and up the Limen Estuary. They attacked the fort at Bonnington, and settled near Appledore. The Norse in East Anglia joined them in the coup, setting up camp at Milton Regis and creating a two-pronged offensive by attacking from the north, and battles raged in the Kentish countryside. Very little ground was given, and after four years they retreated north and south. Regular raids did not stop until the Viking leader Canute ascended to the British throne in 1016, ruling for twenty-six years. He was succeeded by his sons, and then by Edward the Confessor. Particularly notable is the Viking raid on Canterbury in 1011, when they laid siege to the city for three weeks before breaking through the walls and burning down the cathedral. They kidnapped the archbishop, Alphege, who refused to authorise the release of funds for the ransom demand, and was executed. For this, he was elevated to sainthood and is remembered in the names of many churches throughout Kent.

The discovery of a wooden boat at Graveney in 1970 shows that Kentish man was trading widely and had seaworthy ships built in ports such as Faversham. The boat, which was built about AD 930, was a cargo vessel, but could easily have been pressed into service as an early naval craft to move troops about. The cargo of quern stones suggests that the boat was trading with the continent, bringing stones to Kent to be finished before being sold on; the shallow draft allowed it to sail far inland to deliver the goods.

4

THE NORMANS

⚔ 1066–1153 ⚔

Edward the Confessor took the throne after the Norsemen, and ruled for twenty-four years. Before his death, he nominated William, Duke of Normandy, as his successor, but when Edward actually passed away, Harold Godwinson, Earl of Wessex, seized the throne. He was only king for six months, and must have spent much of that time plotting to repel William. Norsemen had attacked Sandwich in January, to draw the attention of Harold before moving northwards to attack the north-east coast of England. Harold had no choice but to take an army and defend his country.

William came to England in October 1066 to claim his throne, bringing 12,000 soldiers to the fight at Hastings, and Harold, after a long march southwards to meet him, was killed. The event is commemorated by the beautiful Bayeux Tapestry, which recent studies claim may have been designed in Canterbury. Scholars have long agreed that the needlewomen who created the tapestry were British, but investigations carried out to identify the designer of the work have shown striking similarities to images held at St Augustine's. It is tempting to believe this, but it is a puzzle that will probably never be solved.

UNCONQUERED

Our Kentish family probably saw Harold's troops marching past towards Hastings, and waited with baited breath to hear the outcome of the battle. As they were part of the humble peasant class, news would have been slow to reach them, and they would initially have been fearful of what the new reign would bring. William I was, after all, descended from the Norsemen who had plundered the county in previous years. Sadly their worries were well founded and the Normans raped and pillaged their way from Hastings, across Romney Marsh to Dover, and up through Kent to London for William I's coronation.

Turning southwards again, William and his troops headed for Dover, but they had not counted on the resistance of the people of Kent. William was stopped at Swanscombe, by Stigande (the Archbishop of Canterbury) and Egelsine (the abbot of St Augustine's). They battled there for three days. Eventually, William saw that he was unlikely to win and negotiated a settlement. Kent became a County Palatine administered by William's half-brother Odo, Bishop of Bayeux, and as such remained unconquered by the Normans. The Kentish motto to this day is 'Invicta' (Unconquered).

The new ruling classes spoke French and this remained the official language of England until 1362; all political and legal work was carried out in French. The clergy used Latin, but our Kentish family spoke Old English, a mixture of their own language, Celtic and Jutish, with a smattering of Norse on top. New French words like 'mutton', 'blouse' and 'liberty' were gradually added, as well as some new French place names, such as Capel-le-Ferne.

This was a time of great growth and prosperity, and the Kentish family were overjoyed that opportunities had arisen for honest manual labour by which means they could keep clothed and fed. Although the Normans were foreign overlords, this was the first time the family had felt safe since the Romans left. The French may have been in charge, but the everyday skills and knowledge came from the people of Kent, who built up the tanning, tile-making, wool production, weaving, iron-working and brewing industries of the county. They felt settled and could look hopefully towards the future.

Building work began in earnest, and construction of Canterbury Castle started around 1070, replacing the motte-and-bailey castle built at the nearby Dane John. Due to its strategic position, near London and conveniently on the way to Dover, it became one of the royal castles of Kent. Canterbury Cathedral was also redesigned at this time, after a devastating fire, and vast quantities of Caen stone were shipped from France for the purpose. The remains of St Augustine's Church rest beneath the nave. Another church was built at Reculver on the site of the old Anglo-Saxon one, which had in turn been built on Roman remains. The church had two distinctive towers, the Two Sisters, which are all that remain and which act as a navigation aid to passing sea traffic.

THE DOMESDAY SURVEY

William I was keen to take stock of his new kingdom, and in 1086 ordered the recording of all land in a Great Survey, information from which was collated into two

volumes later put together as the Domesday Book.
A centre was set up on Penenden Heath, and the landholders of Kent were required to give details of their
estates, including acreage, type of crop grown and any
manufacturing units such as mills or workshops. It is
interesting to note that there were no land *owners*, as
only the king could own land. They also gave information about the number of peasants working on their
land and the number of slaves they held. A study of the
information given shows that only four of the major
landholders were of British descent – all the others had
been replaced by William's French appointees.

There are 377 places recorded in the county of Kent
in Domesday Book, from Dover, Folkestone and Milton
Regis which had approximately 400 households each
(although Milton paid double the tax of Folkestone as
it was a richer area) to 28 towns which were recorded
as having no households of note, including Sandwich,
Woolwich and Margate. The survey was very different
from today's census, where each person is counted – the
Domesday survey counted only the head of each household. Kent was one of the more densely populated areas of
the country, and it is estimated that about 50,000 people
lived there, between 3 and 5 per cent of the country's
total population. Canterbury was the largest town, with
perhaps 2,000 inhabitants, but most people lived around
the river estuaries and in the east of the county; very few
people lived in the Weald, which remained mostly forested.

As the centres of power shifted, the tiny Norman
ruling class sought to consolidate their hold over the local
population by building castles. This was intended to dis-
suade further invasion and to show their strength to the
surrounding villagers. Towns such as Dover, Tonbridge
and Rochester were fortified with enormous castles, as

we can see at Rochester where the castle walls, made of local Kentish ragstone, are 13ft thick. Once completed, the castle at Rochester was gifted to Odo, nominal ruler of Kent. Odo was apparently not grateful, as in 1088 he supported a group of rebel barons in rising up against William Rufus, who inherited the throne on the death of his father, William the Conqueror. For his pains, he was imprisoned in his own castle, and banished to France on his release.

Rochester Castle

Owners of smaller places such as Sutton Valence and Thurnham also felt the need to show their strength and wealth by building castles, albeit smaller than Rochester. Most were built in the traditional motte-and-bailey style, with earthworks and wooden structures, but others, such as Eynsford Castle, were built as enclosure castles, protected by a huge curtain wall around the hall house, with the outbuildings and animal pens inside. Those who could not afford a castle, or who built later, merely constructed a moat around their property, examples of which can be seen at Scotney Castle and Ightham Mote. The spelling of 'mote' in the latter name gives an indication that it was built on the site of an ancient meeting place, and was not named for the moat which now surrounds it.

The beautiful Leeds Castle had been given by King Ethelbert to Ledian, whose name it takes, when it was a hall house within a wooden palisade. Taken over and improved by William the Conqueror, it was upgraded and later completed by Edward I and Eleanor of Castile.

THE ROLE OF THE CHURCH

Churches were also improved, as the old wooden buildings were replaced by stone ones, featuring the iconic squat Norman tower. Examples of Norman architecture can be seen at Barfreston and St Margaret's-at-Cliffe. Builders were keen to reuse stone where they could, to minimise costs, and many Norman churches have worked stone from previous eras incorporated into their fabric. Roman bricks can be seen in the structure of St Mary's at Minster-in-Thanet and St Mary and St Ethelburga Church, Lyminge. The garrison church of St Mary in Castro at Dover also incorporates Roman materials and the church at Luddesdown has Roman tiles in its tower walls.

The Church, with the Archbishop of Canterbury at its head, became a powerful institution, taking control of the daily lives of the populace as well as being an important political force. It built places of worship and gave alms, but also filled its own coffers and those of its ministers. The cathedrals of Rochester and Canterbury were the most impressive buildings, but other minsters, abbeys and churches were also built throughout the county. In fact, almost every village had its own church, built in the distinctive Norman style.

Our Kentish family changed from the old religion to become churchgoers. They liked the cool quietness of the church and enjoyed the calming chant of the clergy, although the services were all in Latin, so they could understand very little, if anything, of the meaning. Attending church was less pleasant in the winter, as the building was unheated and there was no seating for anyone but the very richest patrons.

The Church became the Social Services of the day, providing spiritual guidance, counselling, and help in times of need. Buying up land at a fast rate, the Church built and improved churches, monasteries, schools and hospitals as well as centres for manufacture, agriculture and trade. Underpinning the holy exterior was a powerhouse of commercial enterprise.

One example of the Church's role is the leper hospital that was established at Harbledown and the associated church of St Nicholas, which is still known as the Leper church to local residents. The hospital operated until about 1400 when it became an almshouse, as it is today. St John's Hospital, Canterbury, was established in 1084 for the poor, and St Bartholomew's Hospital was built in Chatham both for the poor and for lepers. Over the coming century, at least 350 hospitals were built across the county, notably in Faversham, New Romney, Dover and Sandwich, and hospitals were in every town by the end of the Norman period.

The two major centres of religion in Kent were, of course, the cathedrals at Canterbury and Rochester, and below these were a hierarchy of churches which spread out like a web across the county. Each tiny village church reported to a larger one, and so on up to the bishop at the cathedral – Maidstone, for example, was termed a 'mother church' with seventeen daughter churches under its purview, and Folkestone had ten.

Other religious institutions such as abbeys, priories and friaries were also being established, with a range of buildings erected on their land to support their communities. Benedictines, Augustinians, Cistercians, Franciscans and Premonstratensians all sought and were granted the right to build religious houses, as did the military orders of the Knights Templar and Knights Hospitaller. As the scale of their building grew, so did their standing in the local community and their power, as employer, purchaser and political force as well as religious leader.

THE BIDDENDEN MAIDS

One local legend tells of the establishment of a custom that is observed in the little village of Biddenden to this day. Conjoined twins were born in 1100 and when they died in 1134, they placed a plot of land in trust to provide for the poor. Almshouses were later built, and rental income from the land provides for the annual distribution of the Biddenden Dole, which has today been translated into a parcel of food for the local poor.

INDUSTRY

Medieval Kent focused on producing grain crops, and was mainly agricultural. However, the geology of the landscape led to the development of three important industries: ironworking, quarrying and cloth making. These three trades were carried out in the west of the country, as the raw materials were to be found in the Weald along with the wood and water needed for power.

The Normans were eager to replace their hastily erected wood and earth castles with stone buildings as soon as possible, and the hard Kentish ragstone was perfect for the job. Sand, clay, chalk and stone were all quarried locally. Ragstone was quarried from Folkestone to Westerham and at Allington, Boughton Monchelsea and Offham.

Iron production had started during the Roman occupation, using local ironstone, and Romney sheep provided wool for cloth which was fulled (cleaned and finished) with local earth. The processing took place in Clothier's Halls, some of which can be identified in the houses of Cranbrook, Biddenden, Staplehurst, Goudhurst, Headcorn and Smarden. Water and timber were readily available in this area to fuel the processes.

Salt production was also an important industry, necessary in the processing and preserving of food. Six large saltines have been found on the Seasalter Flats, of which only one remains in good condition, with the midden heap clearly visible, rising up to 6ft in places. Salt production here stopped in 1325 when the marshes were enclosed and reclaimed.

DAILY LIFE

Our Kentish family kept their home in the country. They liked the rural setting, and towns, although becoming more numerous, were very small by modern standards. There were more opportunities for work in the country and the rustic life suited them. They had farmed the land for generations, being fundamentally self-sufficient and paying rent to the local landowner each year (usually in produce) and giving a tenth (a tithe) to the Church. Visitors can see the wooden enclosure known as a tithe pen at the church of St Augustine at Brookland, where contributions were weighed out, and also the original set of weights used when goods were brought in. Tithe barns, such as that at Lenham, were used to store the goods.

The family sometimes travelled to town to visit the weekly market and sell produce or to buy what they could not make themselves, and they wondered at the commercial warehouses, the official buildings and most of all the number of people on the streets. Luckily, none of them was called to the court or, God forbid, put into gaol. Schools and hospitals were for the rich, and home-schooling and herbal medicine were their lot. They lived on the grains and vegetables they grew, meat from their pigs and the occasional fish from the river. Their oxen were kept to pull the plough, not for meat.

At the beginning of the Norman period, only fourteen markets were held in Kent, but by the end of the fourteenth century, seventy towns and villages had been granted the right to hold a market in their streets. A wide central street used as a High Street is an indication of a Norman marketplace and Wingham is a good example of this practice. In Maidstone, the stalls set up in the middle of the street gradually became more permanent, eventually developing into buildings, and it was in this way that Middle Row developed.

The Kentish family, being farmers, grew but did not grind their own corn, which went to the local mill to be turned into flour, the returned flour being an equivalent weight to the wheat they handed in. Windmills have a long tradition in Kent, but watermills were also in use, as were tide mills, using the power of the tide pushing into rivers and estuaries to power the mill wheel. Hundreds of mills are listed in the Domesday survey, but sadly it does not always record the type of mill.

The width of Wingham High Street shows that it was once used as a market place

The women of the family wove baskets and the men carved out wooden bowls, but if they wanted a pottery dish, as used by the nobility, they had to buy it from the market. There were many potteries in Kent, making goods for local sale and for export. Our Kentish family may have been able to afford some of the smaller dishes and cups for special occasions, but would not have needed the large vessels used for the transport and export of goods, or the roof or floor tiles produced at Tyler Hill in Canterbury, which was particularly famous for its decorated floor tiles. Roof tiles were pegged onto battens, and Kent peg tiles developed to be slightly smaller than those used in the rest of the country, becoming a recognisable speciality of the region.

The reign of William I was followed by that of William Rufus, and he was followed by his brother, who was crowned as Henry I. He named his daughter Matilda as his successor, but William the Conqueror's grandson Stephen of Blois contested this claim. From 1135 to 1154, Britain floundered under a string of invasions and counter-attacks from the two warring cousins. Eventually, Matilda's son Henry ascended the throne as Henry II.

5

THE MAIN PLANTAGENET LINE

⇥ 1154–1399 ⇤

The period of the main Plantagenet line covers just 200 years and yet the reverberations resonate down the halls of time to modern man. The period saw murders and executions, battles and absentee monarchs, but it was also a time of great advances in the areas of law and human rights. The population of the country, although larger than before, only numbered 5 million people, less than the population of London today.

Henry II acceded to the throne in 1154 and one of his first major tasks was to establish the Cinque Port Confederation, a community of Cinque (pronounced 'sink') Ports to defend the south coast. In 1155 he signed a charter which was in effect a contract between five key ports which granted them certain rights and tax benefits in return for an agreement to remain ready at all times to defend the country. The confederation even had its own court at Shepway, whereas residents of other towns were tried at the Shire Court at Penenden Heath.

The ports of Sandwich, Hythe, Romney and Dover, in Kent, and Hastings in Sussex were chosen as key strategic points. Hastings and Dover were each required to provide fifty-seven ships with twenty-one crew each plus one boy, while Sandwich, Hythe and Romney only had to provide five ships. A Warden of the Cinque Ports was chosen, and the office continues today with the official residence being at Walmer Castle.

The first of Henry's improvements to local law was seen in 1156 when magistrates at Canterbury were given the right to hold a Court of Citizens every fifteen days. Again, this was formalised by charter. These groundbreaking changes to British governance seemed to bode well for the reign, and the people of Kent felt much more secure in the understanding that the threat from the French could be easily repelled. However, our churchgoing family was shocked to the core by the next major incident in the history of the county.

MURDER IN THE CATHEDRAL

On 29 December 1170, the Archbishop of Canterbury Thomas Becket was murdered in the cathedral, the same cathedral that the family had visited when in town. Even more disturbing was the news that the murder had been ordered by King Henry. It seemed that nobody was safe.

Thomas Becket had been Archbishop of Canterbury for eight years, and had been chancellor before that, but he had long been arguing with the king. When the king reportedly exclaimed, 'Who will rid me of this turbulent priest?' four knights set off to Canterbury to do just that. It is said that the initial plan involved a little intimidation and a suggestion that Becket leave the country, but it got so out of hand that it is said the stroke which killed him was so violent the tip of the sword broke as it struck the stones of the cathedral floor.

Henry was stunned, as Becket had once been his friend, and as a penance he walked barefoot through the city of Canterbury, being scourged by monks along the way. What a sight for our Kentish family!

A shrine was set up in Canterbury Cathedral which became a place of pilgrimage almost overnight, with Christians travelling for miles to attend the place that suddenly gave rise to miracles. Eastbridge Hospital in Canterbury and St Bart's Hospital in Sandwich were both built in 1190 as hostelries for pilgrims, with their emphasis on the relief of travellers, not the healing of the sick. Although the shrine of Thomas Becket was the most famous place of pilgrimage, there were also others throughout the county, such as the chapel of St Leonard at Saltwood and the Holy Wells at Kemsing and Otford.

The reign of Henry II is marred by the Becket incident, but he made many advances in social justice. In 1166 he established the system of law that we follow today, with local courts and prisons for those awaiting trial. He also established the system of assizes so that decisions were brought about quickly. Henry started to build Dover Castle in 1180 to further fortify the south coast, but did not live to see it finished. He was succeeded by his son Richard I.

Richard I was known as the Lionheart due to his courage in battle. He was a keen soldier and spent most of his reign abroad, fighting in the Holy Land to regain control of contested territory. He travelled through Kent in 1194 on several occasions, most notably when he landed at Sandwich after he had been captured and ransomed by the Austrians on his way home. He allegedly proceeded barefoot to Canterbury to return thanks. He had been accompanied on his crusades by many Kentish men, and they also gave thanks to the Church, this time in the form of monetary donations. Thus, the abbeys, monasteries, nunneries and churches in the area grew richer and even more powerful.

Richard I was succeeded in 1199 by his brother John, whose name is stamped indelibly on the memory of any child as the signatory of the Magna Carta. The charter was signed on 15 June 1215, and it is an almost forgotten fact that the Archbishop of Canterbury, Simon Langton, after whom a local school is named, played an important role in the genesis of the paper that was intended to limit the power of the monarch.

KING LOUIS OF ENGLAND

Although King John had been forced to accept Magna Carta, a band of rebel barons did not trust him to keep to the spirit of the agreement and tried to take the throne of England. The first uprising in 1215 ended in the siege of Rochester Castle where the barons were held for over six weeks. Eventually the soldiers of the Crown dug tunnels underneath the south-eastern tower, and the tower collapsed when the wooden props were deliberately burnt down, allegedly with the fat of forty pigs.

The barons then invited Louis VIII of France to take the throne. He landed at Thanet, and arrived in London in June where he announced that he was King of England. Although never officially crowned, he effectively ruled England for eighteen months, until his battle fleet was repelled at Sandwich on St Bartholomew's Day, 24 August 1217, an event which is remembered annually by the town with a 'bun run' round the church, when children are given currant buns in celebration. Louis departed and Henry III took the throne.

Our Kentish family must have been horrified at the thought of a different French dynasty taking over the country. The ruling class were already mainly French-speaking, but the family feared more drastic changes yet.

MONASTERIES, CHURCHES, HOMES AND HOSPITALS

For the rest of the thirteenth century, Kent saw many new religious houses and places of worship coming to life. The Friars or Aylesford Priory was founded in 1242 when the first Carmelites arrived from the Holy Land. Richard de Grey gave them the land on which to build the priory, which has recently been revitalised. As it was such an important place within the county, the Normans soon built the nearby Medway Bridge for better access.

A good example of a Norman hospital is the Maison Dieu in Faversham, which was commissioned by Henry III in 1234 to serve pilgrims on their way to Canterbury. The flint and timber-framed building is conveniently situated along Watling Street. Unfortunately, many buildings that were associated with the Church were destroyed or repurposed during the Reformation, such as Greyfriars Chapel which is the only building that remains of the first English Franciscan friary built in 1267 in Canterbury. Other buildings have been created from the timbers of these buildings; when Faversham Abbey was destroyed, its timbers were used to create a warehouse on Standard Quay which was given the name Monks Gallery as a nod towards the provenance of the materials. This is one of the oldest warehouses in England.

Monasteries were centres of industry, and sold produce from their gardens to balance the books. One product that was famous throughout the country was Kentish spiced cider, made from the apples from the monastery gardens.

The Normans had brought with them their love of grandeur and a need to stamp their own personality on the land they had conquered. There are hundreds of Norman buildings still in use around the county, including churches, cathedrals, abbeys, hospitals, castles and country houses, even though some of the Norman building work is hidden behind later architectural additions. The Plantagenets continued this building work, which emphasised the divide between the ruling and working classes.

Penshurst Place is one of the most complete examples of fourteenth-century domestic architecture in England. It is a defended manor house, and was later used by Henry VIII as a hunting lodge and for meetings with Anne Boleyn.

One step down from Penshurst Place is Old Soar Manor, Plaxtol, which is part of a stone manor house built around 1290 for a local nobleman. It shows how a house of this nature would have functioned and gives an insight into the life of a rich medieval household. The lord would have provided service to the king in exchange for this land.

Our Kentish family certainly did not live in a house like this, but as part of the villein class they had land of their own, granted to them by the local landowner. Instead of rent, they worked on his estate for three days a week.

A beautiful example of period architecture can be seen in the chapel at Swingate, which is all that remains of the St John's Commandery. Previously used as a farmhouse, this building retains its flint exterior and oak beams much as they would have been when first erected for sisters of the Order of the Knights of St John of Jerusalem.

At Sutton Valance Castle, the ruins of a small stone keep are all that is left of what was once a strongly defended fortification, but Tonbridge Castle is very much in evidence, its current building having replaced the original Norman motte-and-bailey castle on the site. This had been built on a Saxon site which in turn had been built over an Iron Age fort.

DAILY LIFE

Under the Plantagenet kings, our Kentish family lived in a two-roomed house, much the same as during the Norman period. The building had a wooden skeleton, covered with wattle-and-daub but with the added luxury of a wooden floor.

They cooked their food on an open fire (covered ranges were not introduced until much later) and their dinner was stew or pottage containing whatever vegetables, grains or meat were in season. It was a simple diet, mostly vegetarian, with their protein coming from peas and beans, supplemented by the occasional fish or dish of eggs. They were lucky to live in the country as they had access to fresh water and had encouraged a swarm of bees into a hive on their land, so they had a welcome supply of honey. Their goats provided milk and cheese. Inside the house they were gradually accumulating a small collection of heirlooms, including some glazed Roman pottery, an oil lamp and a few cloths to cover their furniture.

THE GREAT FLOOD OF 1287

The Great Flood of 1287 was a shock to everyone and was talked about in the years that followed, much as we talk of the Great Storm of 1987. The coastline of southern Kent was completely altered, creating new areas of land, changing the course of rivers and leaving ports stranded far inland. Old Winchelsea, Sussex, and Broomhill were completely destroyed, and the River Rother was diverted away from New Romney to Rye, which then became the main port in the area. In New Romney, 4ft of silt built up inside St Nicholas' Church, which is now more than a mile inland; an astute visitor will be able to find a mooring ring in front of the church where boats were once tied up. The towns on the north coast were also badly hit, with boats bring driven far inland across the flat wetlands.

ANOTHER ELEPHANT

The year 1255 saw the surprising arrival of an elephant on Kentish shores, not seen there since the time of the Romans. King Louis of France had gifted the elephant to Henry III, and it may have arrived by ship at Dover or Ramsgate, and then walked to London. Alternatively, it may have been shipped from France directly to London, where it lived in the Tower of London, amongst other animals in a royal menagerie. The children of our

Kentish family were lucky, as they caught a glimpse of it as it passed by, and recounted and embellished the story for many weeks afterwards.

THE RHEE WALL

The Rhee Wall is a miracle of medieval engineering, being a run of parallel banks enclosing a canal that travels over 7 miles from New Romney to Appledore. The word 'rhee' is an Old English word for a watercourse, and its purpose was to channel water from inland Appledore out to the sea at New Romney, clearing silt as it went. Despite the best efforts of the medieval engineers, the silt nevertheless built up and after 100 years the canal dried out. The Walland Marsh, to the south-west of the wall, was at that time owned by successive Archbishops of Canterbury and the place names St Boniface's, St Peckham's and so on reflect this.

EXPULSION OF THE JEWS

Our Kentish family were sad to hear that some of their neighbours had to leave when Edward the Confessor expelled the whole Jewish community from England, signing an Act of Parliament to that effect in 1290. They moved to the continent, and did not return until the time of Oliver Cromwell.

The fourteenth century was hard for the Kentish family, with a regular change of kings, revolts and the Black Death. The century had started well, and in 1320 Margate Harbour was built to carry Kentish produce such as barley, fish and fresh vegetables to London faster than it could be transported overland. Provender House was another new building in Faversham and was built in 1342 for Lucas de Vienne, the chief archer to Edward, the Black Prince, and is currently the home of Her Highness Princess Olga Romanov.

SHEEP AND OWLS

In 1331, migrant cloth workers from Flanders were invited by Edward III to England and settled in Tenterden, Biddenden, Cranbrook and Staplehurst, where both water for the mills and the fuller's earth used for removing grease from the wool were readily available. Fine, high-quality fuller's earth was actually so essential to the process that its export was forbidden, lest it help rival manufacturers. The Flemish workers shared their skills in weaving and fulling cloth with the local people, the industry grew and Wealden broadcloth became sought after throughout the country. Kentish broadcloth was 58in wide and each piece had to be between 30 and 34yd long and weigh 66lb. The weight regulation ensured that the cloth was of good, thick quality. The cloth was dyed many colours, but a certain shade of grey was particularly popular and eventually became widely known as Kentish Grey.

The production of wool became an important source of wealth, so when a ban on the export of woollen cloth to the continent, where prices were higher, was imposed a new trade emerged: smuggling. The men who carried bundles of cloth through the Weald and the Romney Marshes to the ports communicated by mimicking the calls of owls, and so were called 'owlers'. Another Kentish dialect phrase is 'black robin', which refers to highwaymen.

THE BLACK DEATH

By 1347 the life of our Kentish family was going well. They had settled in a prosperous and expanding village, attended the local church and had regular employment. In 1348, however, their lives were rocked by the bubonic plague, which became infamous as the Black Death or the Great Pestilence. Outbreaks of plague were not unknown, but this was a particularly virulent strain which killed up to 50 per cent of the population. Fields were left untended, streets were deserted and food became scarce. The population of England had reached a million at the beginning of the century, but by the end of the Plantagenet period in 1399 it had fallen to half that number, due principally to the effects of the Black Death.

Kent has many reminders of this sad time but two of the most thought-provoking are St Leonard's Church, Hythe which has a large ossuary in the crypt, in which are stored over 1,000 skulls and 8,000 thigh bones, reputedly victims of the plague, and the Lost Village of Dode from which the inhabitants were all lost during the years of the plague. The only building still standing is the deconsecrated church, which is currently in private hands and is available as a venue for weddings.

LOOKER'S HUTS

The Black Death brought about another change in the landscape of Kent. Romney Marsh had long been used for sheep farming, with the hardy Romney sheep able to survive well on the salt marshes, but after the plague swathes of land lay untended and absentee landlords bought up the land and populated it with sheep, employing independent shepherds to look after them. These 'lookers' might have half a dozen flocks to care for and during lambing season they lived out in the 'looker's huts' that can be seen in the area today. There were once perhaps 350 of these tiny one-roomed cottages on the marsh, each made of brick with Kent peg tiles on the roof, but today there are barely a handful. One window and a fireplace to warm your dinner and any motherless lambs were all that was needed. There is a local recipe for Looker's Pie that includes mutton and vegetables, but shepherds would also have fried up the docked tails of the growing lambs, which were removed to prevent infection. Waste not, want not.

THE PEASANTS ARE REVOLTING!

A writ in 1351 had set wages at pre-plague levels, limiting what could be charged for goods, and had outlawed the giving of alms to beggars. The Crown exacerbated matters by introducing a poll tax in 1377, 1379 and 1380. There was more work for fewer people and they were being paid less for that work. This was certainly something for the Kentish family to discuss with their friends and co-workers.

By 1381 the Kentish family and their peers had had enough. In June, they joined with other rebels to release John Ball from Maidstone Prison, where he had been imprisoned for repeatedly advocating a classless society, and travelled to Penenden Heath to plan a revolution. After capturing Rochester Castle and freeing the prisoners, the men were joined by Walter (Wat) Tyler, from Essex. Wat led the peasant throng (reportedly up to 100,000 strong) through Kent to London where they destroyed property, including John of Gaunt's palace, and murdered many innocent tradesmen. King Richard II initially agreed terms, but soon afterwards the terms were forgotten and Wat Tyler was hanged, drawn and quartered, along with other rebel leaders. Luckily, a general amnesty was issued at Christmas for other participants, and the men from our Kentish family used the back roads and byways to travel quietly home.

The revolution seemed to have achieved little and the men felt lucky to be alive. However, things did gradually improve as the king had seen the passionate nature and strength of the lower classes and treated them with more respect and he did repeal the poll tax. Several were not happy with the outcome and, feeling more could be achieved, marched on Linton and Maidstone in September 1382, but they were quickly quashed.

Our Kentish family did not join this second rebellion. They may have felt that the earthquake of May that year was a warning from on high. The bell tower of Canterbury Cathedral was damaged, as were several nearby buildings, and the bells rang out across the city.

Life returned to normal, and the revolt was pushed to the back of people's minds. Kent gained a new Member of Parliament, one Geoffrey Chaucer who was elected in 1386. He had earlier been in the Customs Service, which would not have made him popular, and he served as an MP for only one year before retreating into semi-retirement to write *The Canterbury Tales*.

At the end of the reign of Richard II, life was very different from the preceding medieval lifestyle. The peasant class had shown its strength, but the divide between the very rich and the very poor had widened. Richard had introduced the term 'your majesty' for himself, instead of the previous term 'your grace' or 'your highness', and he demanded more obeisance than ever before. Some scholars have suggested that the current population of the UK has up to 80 per cent Plantagenet blood running through its veins. Whatever the truth of the matter, Richard was deposed by his cousin, who became Henry VI, and the main Plantagenet line ended in 1399.

A Looker's Hut on Romney Marsh

6

THE HOUSE OF LANCASTER

⚜ 1399–1461 ⚜

The House of Lancaster ruled England for less than 100 years. However, it was an influential period and our Kentish family once again felt the need to champion the rights of the lower classes against the ruling elite of the country.

THE BATTLE OF AGINCOURT

Many towns in Kent such as Eccles, Stelling Minnis and Sandwich have areas of land named The Butts. These were areas where medieval archers honed their skills in preparation for battle. From 1252, all men between the ages of 15 and 60 had been required to own a bow with arrows and to know how to use it, although interestingly those people who lived in the royal forests had to use blunt arrows to discourage them from shooting the game which belonged by divine right to the king.

Our Kentish family had several sons, and they all had to be armed.

Edward III had increased the burden on the men of the land when he had passed the Archery Law in 1363, which commanded the practice of archery on Sundays and holidays by all men, and this law had not been rescinded. This was the only rest day of the week for people of the lower classes and it had been taken from them. Even boys as young as 7 were required to attend practice, although the adults tried to make it more interesting for them by running competitions and leagues.

The Battle of Agincourt (1415) was one of the major battles during the Hundred Years War (which finally ended in 1453) and has gone down in history as a time of great bravery among the victorious English. Once again, the people of Kent were involved. Among others, three men-at-arms and nine archers from Stelling Minnis accompanied their squire Sir Nicholas de Haute to join Henry V's army in France.

The English were outnumbered six to one, but the archers could shoot twelve armour-piercing arrows a minute and it was said that the skies over Agincourt were black with arrows. All that practice had paid off.

DAILY LIFE

Everyday life was increasingly comfortable as the centuries passed, and although our Kentish family's home had not changed from the basic wattle-and-daub structure, it was no longer just one large room around an open fireplace. Like many other houses, they had private rooms and their land was marked out from that of their neighbours by a hedge or ditch. Their furniture was basic, but was kept clean, and their few possessions were either proudly displayed on shelving or carefully tucked away in a wooden chest. They ate from pewter plates and had a few glazed pots for special occasions.

The family had benefited from the Black Death. Although sorry to see so many of their neighbours perish in the disaster, and losing some family members themselves, it did mean that more land became available to buy. The population of England had halved in the past 200 years, falling from almost 4 million to barely over 2 million, and the family were able to increase their 20 acres by another 10 acres. They were now free tenants, and as such did not owe as much to the local landowner as serfs and lower peasants.

As the family became more comfortably off, their diet improved and more fruit and vegetables were included along with the meat, bread and dairy produce of the previous century. They visited the market to trade excess produce and to buy in items they needed. People on the coast had a ready supply of fish and shellfish from the sea and those inland ate freshwater fish or eels. The consequence of this was that prices rose, and with them the level of taxation.

JACK CADE'S REBELLION

Things came to a head in 1450 when Jack Cade, an Irishman living in Kent, drew together a group of small-holders and travelled to London to protest, carrying a manifesto entitled 'The Complaint of the Poor Commons of Kent'. They rioted in the streets of London, held a kangaroo court and executed the Lord High Treasurer, before rampaging once more through the streets of London.

A medieval archer was required to practise at least once a week

Although the rebellion was popular with many people outside the capital, the Londoners objected and drove them from the city. Jack Cade was later executed, but it is said that the words of 'The Complaint' formed the basis of the revolt of the House of York when the Wars of the Roses started just five years later between the House of Lancaster, whose emblem was a red rose, and the House of York, whose emblem was a white rose.

THE FRENCH INVADE SANDWICH

The rule of the House of Lancaster ended with a bombshell for Kent. English ships had been harrying the coast of France for many years, and the French, seeing the country weakened by internal struggles, took their chance. In August 1457, a large French fleet waited off-shore until the tides allowed and then sailed into the harbour of Sandwich. Although the town is now some 2 miles from the sea, it was then a prosperous port. The French burned and looted the town, which was severely damaged, and the battle raged until 5.30 p.m. that evening when reinforcements arrived from nearby Cinque Port towns. One of the men killed was the mayor of Sandwich, and the current incumbent always wears black robes in remembrance of this event.

7

THE HOUSE OF YORK

⚡ 1461–1485 ⚡

This twenty-four-year period of our history is once again one of the most memorable. Who hasn't heard of the Princes in the Tower, 'A horse, a horse! My kingdom for a horse!', William Caxton or the king in the car park?

Luckily for our Kentish family, the Wars of the Roses took place much further north than their little corner of England. Rumour and counter-rumour circulated wildly as the battles raged between the two royal houses, each vying for control of the country. Unlike previous wars on the continent and further afield in the Holy Land, kings, soldiers and their followers did not travel through Kent to the ports, so information was limited.

As Edward IV's reign began, the troubles carried on, but still at a distance from Kent. His son, Edward V, reigned for only one year before he was imprisoned in the Tower of London by his Uncle Richard. The Duke of Gloucester helped Richard III take the throne, although he lost it at the Battle of Bosworth Field in 1485. The famous cry of 'my kingdom for a horse' was later penned by Shakespeare to describe the mood of the moment. It was Richard's body that was found in the car park in Leicester in 2012. He was succeeded by Henry VII, who founded the House of Tudor.

BUILDINGS OF THE YORKIST PERIOD

This short period in Kentish history is hard to define. Building work continued and many houses that had been started were brought to completion or near-completion.

One example is Chilham Village Hall, a timber-framed fifteenth-century tithe barn once used to store the 'tithe' – 10 per cent of each harvest given to the Church. It has been updated and is today used by members of the local community for a variety of purposes. The inside shows the dark oak beams and whitewashed infilled walls that one associates so readily with this style of architecture. Another such building is Stoneacre House near Maidstone, which is a beautiful example of a fifteenth-century Wealden hall house, owned by the National Trust. The half-timbered property would have belonged to a yeoman of higher standing than our Kentish family.

Domestic architecture in the west of Kent was dominated by Wealden hall houses, four-roomed, two-storey buildings with wattle-and-daub walls and a thatched roof. A good example is Bayleaf Farm Hall from Chiddingstone, which has been restored to its original construction and moved to the Weald and Downland Museum near Chichester, where it is enjoyed daily by historians and other visitors.

Stoneacre House, Maidstone

THE KENT DITCH

The Romans had started to reclaim land at Romney Marsh with sea defences being added and drainage systems installed. The canal called the Rhee Wall had started to silt up since it was built, and a drainage channel described as the Kent Ditch, which forms part of the border between Kent and East Sussex, was excavated. Another area the Romans had reclaimed was the marshy area on the north Kent coast near Rainham.

WILLIAM CAXTON

William Caxton, who had been born in Tenterden, was almost 40 at the beginning of the rule of the House of York. He travelled widely on the continent and brought back with him details of Johannes Gutenberg's printing press, which he had seen in Cologne, Germany. He had already collaborated with Colard Mansion in Bruges to produce the first ever book and in 1476 he travelled back through Kent to London. Here, he set up the first British printing press and printed books in the English language, for the benefit of the people as a whole, not just for scholars. One of the books he printed was *The Canterbury Tales*, written by man of Kent Geoffrey Chaucer and produced in 1477. While most of Caxton's work was carried on outside Kent, men of Kent still like to tell visitors that he was 'one of theirs'.

BRICKS AND TILES

Industry was catching up with agriculture as the main source of employment in the county, providing year-round rather than seasonal work. Men who took a job in a local manufacturing plant for the slack winter period often stayed there when spring came, glad of the regular wages.

Kent has been famous for its high-quality brick and tile manufacture since Roman times. The success of the industry is due to the type of chalk and brick-earth deposits within the Kent landscape. The name 'peg tile' applies to a plain clay tile suspended from the top edge of a wooden lath or batten so as to overlap two courses below, held in place by a small wooden peg. Canterbury has its own particular version of the peg tile: the 'Kent peg' is half an inch smaller than tiles from other parts of the country and has a slightly irregular shape, a mix of warm orange-red hues, and a varied texture.

The House of York ended with Richard III.

8

THE EARLY TUDORS

⊰ 1485–1558 ⊱

The Tudor period was a tempestuous time, and Kent was privy to much of it. Kings and queens developed a fondness for Kent with its pretty countryside and its proximity to the continent, travelling widely through the landscape either to visit or on their way to one of the ports.

Henry VII, the first Tudor king, admired Canterbury Cathedral, and the Bell Harry Tower, which houses the cathedral bells, was erected in 1498 to enhance and embellish the building. The entrance to the cathedral from the Butter Market is through the imposing Christ Church Gate, which was commissioned by Henry in 1502. It shows his own coat of arms along with that of the golden couple, the king's son Prince Arthur and his wife Katherine of Aragon. Sadly Arthur died before he could ascend the throne and Katherine married his brother Henry.

Ironically, it was at about this time that Thomas Boleyn inherited Hever Castle from his father and moved down from Norfolk with his wife and three young children, among them his daughter Anne, who was destined to become Queen of England. In another twist of irony, Hever was later given to Anne of Cleves alongside other properties as part of her divorce settlement and she lived there until her death her death at Chelsea Old Manor in 1557.

It is always interesting to look across the 22-mile width of the English Channel from Dover to Calais and remember that the latter was once under English control. Henry VIII was the last English king to hold the title of King of France and it was he who lost the greater part of the port of Calais. On the other hand, it was under the reign of the Tudor monarchs that England started to explore and trade more widely, and with hindsight we can see that this was the start of the British Empire.

Where Sandwich shows the architecture and street layout of a medieval town, Chiddingstone shows the architecture of a Tudor village, with its row of half-timbered houses with their upper storeys overhanging the main street, financed in large part by the Streatfield family who built and owned Chiddingstone Castle. However, the run of jettied houses in Strand Street in Sandwich is thought to be the longest block of timber-framed houses still in use in England.

Our Kentish family had risen to become part of the yeoman class, neither hugely wealthy nor horribly poor. In the Tudor period, 90 per cent of the country was engaged in agriculture, and our family was no exception. Their house had changed very little from the previous era, and their diet may even have got worse as crops failed and prices rose. They tried to keep out of political discussions and worked hard, keeping to the normal six-day working week, feeling lucky that they had enough animals to provide eggs, milk and cheese as well as the odd bite of meat.

In 1509 the throne passed to Henry VII's second son, Henry VIII. Unlike his older brother Arthur, he was brash and had a fiery temper; he arguably had more of an effect on Britain than any other king.

THE HOLY MAID OF KENT

Elizabeth Barton was born in Aldington and worked as a servant girl in Court Lodge Farmhouse, a manor house which had been bought by Henry VII and much extended. About 1525 she became ill and as a result of this had times when she fell into trances that reportedly contained religious visions. Three years later she entered a nunnery in Canterbury, the visions did not stop and she became known as the Holy Maid of Kent. Unfortunately for her, the visions told her that she should warn Henry VIII that if he divorced Katherine of Aragon and married Anne Boleyn, the vengeance of God would fall upon him and he would die within months. She did manage to gain an audience with Henry and warned him of her prophecies. Not surprisingly, she was tried for treason, found guilty and executed at Tyburn in April 1534. She is remembered as the only woman whose head was displayed on a spike on London Bridge. Thomas More lost his head the same year, and it was brought to Kent by his daughter, where it is buried at St Dunstan's Church in Canterbury.

THE REFORMATION

Thomas Hitton of Maidstone is considered the first English martyr of the Reformation, although he died before Henry VIII declared himself the head of the Church. He was arrested at Gravesend for smuggling in a psalter printed in English and was accused of heresy. He was burned at the stake in Maidstone in February 1530.

In 1534 Henry VIII appointed himself 'The Supreme Head on Earth of the Church', thus breaking ties with

Rome and enabling him to dictate the way the Church was run in England. Under Roman Catholic law, the pope was the supreme leader, reporting directly to God, with kings and queens falling below him in the hierarchy. Henry VIII broke from this doctrine, declaring that the monarch was the overall head of the Church, while allowing that the Archbishop of Canterbury was the spiritual leader. His new era of religion in the country also saw him dissolve the monasteries.

Due to its long association with Christianity, Kent was home to many of the most beautiful monasteries in the country and they were all razed to the ground, damaged beyond repair or forfeit to the Crown. Our Kentish family were alarmed when they heard of men rampaging through their local church, knocking down statues and collecting the gold and silverware. They were even more shocked when the stained-glass windows were smashed or removed and the associated administrative buildings were gifted to prominent civil servants or sold to the highest bidder. Canterbury Cathedral suffered greatly during this time as it had been the home of Benedictine monks since the tenth century, and when the monastery was dissolved, responsibility for the cathedral was taken over by a group of clergy under the title 'the Chapter of Canterbury'.

Henry's reforms, however, were not all bad, for alongside the dissolution of the monasteries, he introduced the use of bibles and prayer books written in plain English, insisting that each parish church had a copy. Previously, religious books had been written in Latin and their messages translated to the congregation by the clergy. Henry believed that everyone should be able to read the Word of God and he encouraged discussions on religious matters.

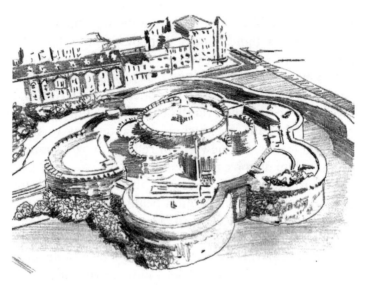

Deal Castle, one of Henry VIII's device forts

FORTS AND FORTIFICATIONS

Henry VIII was plagued with insecurities and obsessed with fortifying the country. His attentions focused mainly on Kent and the south coast, hoping to repel attacks from the French, with whom relations were quickly deteriorating.

When the pope excommunicated Henry, the danger of invasion became a reality. Forts were built at Gravesend and Milton (near Sittingbourne) with cannon matching the two at Tilbury on the other side of the Thames, thus protecting London, and Henry also repaired and strengthened the castle at Queenborough. In 1539, he ordered a series of 'device forts' at Deal, Walmer, Sandgate and Sandown, and used Deal in particular as a stop-off point on his way to and from the continent. These forts were built in the shape of a Tudor rose with two concentric outer walls in a petal shape and a deep moat for further protection. The 'petals' were in fact gun emplacements, and the structures had been built to house cannon rather than as forts to withstand siege conditions.

The device forts were situated on the east coast as Henry believed this to be the most likely point of invasion. As Julius Caesar had found, the shallow, shingly beaches were much more welcoming that the steep cliffs at Dover. Sandgate was built to provide protection for the stretch of coast between Dover and Folkestone. Sandown can be seen today as little more than a pile of rubble and Sandgate has been repurposed as a Martello tower, but Deal and Walmer are regularly open to the public.

Each hundred in Kent was ordered to provide men to man the forts, but few came forward, and money was not available to provide sufficient arms or training. With hindsight, the county was lucky an invasion never came. A quintain or tilting pole can be seen on the village green at Offham, which would have been used for practice against the threat of possible invasion and is reflected in other villages across the county.

SHIPS AND SHIPYARDS

Henry VIII was also the father of the Royal Navy. The royal dockyard at Woolwich, which was then in Kent, had been started in 1512, and he also developed the site at Deptford, as both were near his palace at Greenwich. Henry was also concerned about the silting up of the harbours where his ships were moored and one of his responses was the sea defence works known as Mole Rocks, which was installed to slow the silting of the port of Dover. Henry had inherited only five royal ships from his father, but by the time he died he had forty.

In 1547 Henry established a storehouse at Chatham to house supplies for the royal warships, which was later developed into Chatham Dockyard. By the 1570s it was fully established and recognised as a royal dockyard. Timber for the ships was sourced locally, and several pubs still go by the name 'The Hook and Hatchet', which is a reference to the badge of the chief petty officer shipwright who had authority to order timber-felling for wood to build and fit out ships.

The village of Smallhythe is situated 10 miles inland, but was once an important port. Smallhythe Place was called Port House and was home to the harbour master. Built in 1515, it is a fabulous example of an early sixteenth-century house and was built on the banks of the River Rother, and was then a royal shipyard. Henry V (Henry VIII's great-grandfather) oversaw the building of the first 1,000-ton warship, the *Jesus*, which was used in the fifteenth century for scouting and raiding. Later, the river began to silt up and new shipyards were built. The last ship to be built at Smallhythe was the *Great Gallyon* in 1546, which was commissioned by Henry VIII. At 300 tons, she was the last of the great ships, the last royal commission for Smallhythe and the last large vessel to be built there.

Sadly, this period also saw the decline of the Cinque Port Federation, which had been considered so important by Henry's father and grandfather.

TUDOR BUILDINGS

Henry VIII thought a great deal of his own importance and much building work took place in Kent to reflect this.

One such building was the Margate Tudor House, which is thought to be one of the oldest of its kind in Kent. It was built in 1525 as a yeoman farmer's house and has been granted Grade II listed building status, its design falling between the medieval practice of living in a one-roomed hall house and the Tudor-style two-storey buildings. It is remarkable for its period in that it was designed with two chimneys, and restoration work carried out on the house in 1951 was notable as it used 86 per cent reclaimed Tudor materials.

At the beginning of his reign, Henry updated and beautified Leeds Castle for his wife Katherine of Aragon and it became a royal palace. He stayed there with Katherine in 1520 on his way to the Field of the Cloth of Gold, and again in 1544 with his last wife, Catherine Parr. Legend has it that he also stopped in the village of Chartham to have his horses re-shod at the blacksmith's on The Green. Records show that the retinue incorporated 1,637 horses, and one assumes that they were re-shod in rotation, not en masse.

Following the dissolution of Dartford Priory, Henry VIII chose the site to construct a manor house for his personal use. In 1545, this venue became one of the most politically important sites in Tudor England, as the Privy Council would meet here. Anne of Cleves was given the manor house as part of her divorce settlement by Henry, and lived there between 1553 and 1557. Today, only the gatehouse remains.

Although Fordwich has never boasted more than a few hundred inhabitants, its right to style itself a town dates from 1184, when King Henry II granted it a merchant guild charter, as it was the nearest that ships could get to Canterbury when sailing up the Stour. It therefore became not only an inland port, but also

England's smallest town. The town hall, built in 1544, is still used on a regular basis by the town council for their meetings.

THE GARDEN OF ENGLAND

It was Henry VIII who asked his fruiterer to establish over 100 acres of cherry orchard at Teynham and to keep the fruit exclusively for the use of the court. The Kentish Red cherry is smaller than the Morello we see so often in the shops and bright red in colour. Apple and pear orchards were also established and it is said that it was Henry who first used the phrase 'The Garden of England' to refer to Kent, a phrase which persists in common use today, although it is not currently the country's leading producer. Kent is home to the National Fruit Collection at nearby Brogdale, and contains many old varieties including the Costard and Pearmain which were brought to England by the Normans.

When Henry VIII died in 1547, his 9-year-old son became King Edward VI. He only ruled for six years, but he is remembered for the rigorous enforcement of his father's religious ideas.

Joan Boucher, sometimes called Joan of Kent – not to be confused with the mother of Richard II who went by the same name – advocated religious reform. She was born near Romney and grew up with strong Anabaptist ideals, coming to Canterbury to preach. Like so many dissenters of the period, she was arrested, tried for heresy and burned at the stake in 1550.

Mary I took the throne in 1553, and the next five years were violent and unsettled. Mary disagreed with the establishment of the Church of England and returned

England to the Roman Catholic faith. During her reign, she ordered the execution of over 300 dissenters, which earned her the nickname Bloody Mary.

Mary was not a popular queen and in 1554 Sir Thomas Wyatt, a landowner from Kent and staunch Protestant, made a bid to stop Mary from marrying Philip of Spain and possibly to depose her altogether. He started at Allington Castle, near Maidstone, and within days had amassed a group of 4,000 supporters. The 600 men sent from London to prevent the rebellion joined the band and marched with them towards London. Wyatt made his way along the north coast of Kent, but was stopped at Deptford. He circled round and entered the city at Kingston, but even the size of his following was not enough and they were defeated. Wyatt and 150 rebels were executed and their lands, titles and money forfeit. The town of Maidstone was stripped of its royal charter for its part in the uprising. The fact that these were restored by Elizabeth I when she came to the throne was little comfort to those, like our Kentish family, who had lost relatives.

KENTISH MARTYRS

Mary reigned until 1558, and more Kentish men were to lose their lives during this period. In 1555 eighteen Kentish men were burned at the stake in Canterbury in the area of Martyr's Field. Five men and women were burned at locations across the county in 1556, another thirteen lost their lives the same way in 1557, and five more died in 1588. In total, about seventy Kentish men and women were burned during what are referred to as the Marian Persecutions.

The second event that overshadows Mary's reign was that she lost Calais. Lacking the military resources to fight back, Calais, as important to England as Gibraltar is to the UK, was lost to the French in 1557, just ten months before her death. Despite the fact that she married, she died childless and her sister Elizabeth became the second of Henry VIII's daughters to be queen, returning the nation to Anglican worship.

Leeds Castle, favourite of kings and queens from the time of William I

9

THE ELIZABETHANS

⊰ 1558–1603 ⊱

The age of Elizabeth I was one of great exploration and expansion, both of the British Empire and of the minds of the citizens. The population of England had shot up to almost 3 million, a million more than at the beginning of the Tudor period.

Elizabeth was 25 when she came to the throne and she reigned for forty-five years until her death aged 69. During this time, Elizabeth passed through Kent on several occasions, both while on royal progress, when she visited stately homes and met her subjects, and also when travelling to and from the port of Dover. Of course, she had also been born in Greenwich, which was at that time part of the county of Kent, and as such she was a Kentish Maid.

Our Kentish family was happy with the restoration of the Church of England after the horrors of the reign of Queen Mary and looked forward to a time of peace and prosperity. They were even happier at the introduction of seating in churches. Sermons were getting longer, and it was a luxury to be able to sit down instead of standing throughout the service. Towards the end of the reign, some churches installed the very modern box pews, an example of which can be seen at St Clement's Church on Romney Marsh.

ELIZABETHAN INDUSTRY

Silk weaving came to Canterbury in 1560 and market gardening arrived in Sandwich at the same time, brought over with immigrant workers. Market gardeners from the Low Countries specialised in cabbages, carrots and celery, and they brought their skills to north-east Kent. As their businesses grew, they moved nearer to London and into north-west Kent. The weaving industry at Canterbury also prospered, so that by 1660 over 2,000 people were employed in the trade.

England and Flanders had traded in cloth for hundreds of years, and some Dutch immigrants had already settled in Sandwich. As the port began to silt up during the reign of Elizabeth, Dutch workers sought permission to establish a larger community in the area and in 1561 Elizabeth granted 300 people the right to live and work in Sandwich, providing they created types of cloth not then made in England. They brought with them their own culture and traditions, and today hundreds of beautiful Dutch-style buildings can be seen across the east of Kent.

Linked to the textile industry was the mining of copperas on the north Kent coast. Copperas (hydrated ferrous sulphate) was used in the textile industry as a dye fixative and in the manufacture of ink, and there was a large plant at Whitstable from 1565. The remains of a sixteenth-century ship were found at Tankerton in April 2017, which is currently in the process of being excavated, and which promises a detailed insight not only into the shipbuilding industry but also into the copperas industry. It is the only known surviving medieval shipwreck in the south-east, preserved in the dense London clay.

The iron industry, which had been started, not surprisingly, in the Iron Age, matured in the Elizabethan period, and was centred in the Weald where there was ample fuel for the kilns and furnaces. In 1573, there were eight furnaces operating in the area, with Lamberhurst being one of the centres of operation. Furnace ponds and bays remain at Horsmonden, Lamberhurst and Cowden.

In 1575, the Walloons came to Kent as refugees, fleeing from the Catholic Inquisition in Belgium. Referred to as the Strangers, they were permitted by the Crown to settle in Canterbury. They brought with them their skills in weaving wool, and wove beautiful cloth from the wool spun by local women and girls from the fleece of the Romney sheep.

In 1589, Elizabeth granted John Spilman a licence to make white writing paper and he established the first English paper mill in Dartford. The family ran the mill until the mid-1700s. Other mills followed, at Ayesford, Maidstone, Canterbury and elsewhere.

QUEEN ELIZABETH VISITS KENT

Queen Elizabeth visited Kent many times during her reign, often staying at great houses like Penshurst Place. A royal progress was no small affair, as the queen, her belongings, her ladies and servants and their belongings all had to travel together. This could amount to 500 or more horse-drawn carts, following the faster riders on horseback. It was rather like travelling to a B&B where nothing is provided, so Elizabeth took her bedding, dishes and kitchen equipment as well as any documents that she was working on at the time and of course her clothing and jewels. Even on horseback, the party only travelled about 10 miles a day.

One particularly well-documented visit is the one she made to Sandwich in 1573.The people of Sandwich pulled out all the stops and when she arrived the townspeople threw flowers at her feet, wrote poems and prepared a banquet of 150 different dishes. The queen loved the banquet and asked for several of the dishes to be carried back to her lodgings – high praise indeed. It is thought that she was staying at the house identified as The King's Lodgings, which had offered hospitality to Henry VIII when he visited.

ELIZABETHAN BUILDINGS

Elizabeth I reigned for less than fifty years, and yet the buildings which were erected during her time on the throne are iconic, taking their influence from many cultures across Europe. There were no new palaces built during this period, but imposing red-brick houses with iconic Elizabethan chimneys multiplied.

The Faversham covered market place which is even now used every week by market traders was built in 1574, although the Guildhall above it was added at a later date, the arched pillars of grey stone providing shade for the produce on market days. Knole House, later the home of Vita Sackville-West and erected a few years later, is said to be a calendar house with 365 rooms, 52 staircases, 12 entrances and 7 courtyards.

Eastgate House, Rochester

Eastgate House in Rochester was built in the 1590s and is a designated Grade I listed building. Built as a town-house, it still dominates the High Street. Also in Rochester is the Six Poor Travellers House, built in 1586, the ground floor of which has been converted into a museum. It was founded by the local MP Richard Watts, who left money in his will for the benefit of six poor travellers, each of whom, according to a plaque on the outside of the building, would be given lodging and 'entertainment' for one night before being sent on his way with 4*d* in his pocket.

During this time, several buildings in Kent were decorated with pargetting work. Normally associated with Essex and Suffolk, this decorated plasterwork is a step up from plain walls, but significantly cheaper than carved stone. The building in Canterbury High Street labelled Queen Elizabeth's Guest Chamber has impressive pargetting visible on the front and it is here that she supposedly entertained the Duc d'Alençon in 1573. An example of painted plaster decoration can be seen in Bank Street, Maidstone, although that on the upper floors has been removed.

There is a rare surviving example of a Tudor garden at Northbourne Court. The ground was cleverly built up in terraces so that visitors could see over the garden walls to the countryside beyond.

SPANISH ARMADA

Mary I and her Spanish husband Philip had both been Catholic, and when Elizabeth I took the throne, Spain was worried. Philip put together an armada (fleet) of 130 ships, planning to pick up more troops from the Netherlands and then invade Britain so he could convert it back to Catholicism.

Elizabeth needed plans in place to repel an invasion and in 1570 she upgraded the system of beacons that ran across the south of the country from the coast to London, in preparation for enemy attack. Kent was once again in the front line and was ordered to provide 1,500 men along with 9,000lb of gunpowder and 900lb of lead. Thirty beacons were installed in Kent, growing in sophistication from low bonfires to become baskets of pitch-soaked combustibles on a tall pole.

After several delays, the Spanish Armada eventually set sail in 1588, and was reportedly heading for Margate. Luckily, the fleet was stopped at Calais, where the Spanish ships were too large to enter the harbour, and a fierce sea battle ensued, which lasted several days. Our Kentish family lived near enough to Dover at the time to be able to stand on the cliffs and watch the fires of the battle raging across the water, before saying a quick prayer and going home glad that this time an invasion had been prevented. There were further rumours of invasion throughout the 1590s, but none materialised.

PIRATES AND PRIVATEERS

Once the threat of the Spanish invasion had lessened, many fishermen and sailors saw an opportunity to make some extra money plundering Spanish ships. Queen Elizabeth recognised this practice as a legitimate enterprise and issued licences, called 'letters of marque'. One sailor who benefited was John Ward, who was born in Faversham and rose to fame as a Robin-Hood-like swashbuckling privateer raiding the vessels of Catholic countries while sparing those from Britain. When James I came to the throne and rescinded the licences, John Ward continued to take Spanish ships, but being now outside the law he was labelled a pirate. He worked in the waters around Britain and in the Mediterranean, inspiring ballads and stories as his fame grew. Towards the end of his life, he accepted the teachings of Islam and changed his name to Issouf Reis, dying at the age of 70 in Tunisia.

DAILY LIFE

Daily life had not improved as it had in previous decades, but visitors from the continent noted that the poor in

England were much better off than their counterparts across the Channel. Prices had risen steeply, although the self-sufficient Kentish family were protected in some measure. By bartering instead of selling goods, they kept their standard of living relatively stable. Agriculture remained the major industry in Kent, and a labourer earnt about 7s a week.

The family had a scare in 1595 when the bubonic plague visited east Kent again, and although it was a much less virulent strain than that which caused the Black Death, the larger towns were badly affected. In Canterbury, quarantine tents were erected in Dane John Gardens and in 1597 the plague hit smaller places like Sandwich and Cranbrook.

EDUCATION

As the religious establishments which had previously provided teaching for the young men of the county had disappeared during the Reformation, local entrepreneurs and trade guilds started to build schools of their own. Grammar schools sprang up at Cranbrook, Tonbridge, Sutton Valence and Dartford.

One of the people who benefited from The King's School at Canterbury was Christopher 'Kit' Marlowe. After leaving the school he attended Cambridge University and then produced an extraordinary series of plays including *Tamburlaine* and *Doctor Faustus*, while at the same time reputedly acting as a spy for Queen Elizabeth. If he was spy, Marlowe must have travelled repeatedly through Kent going to and from the continent, but his life was cut short when, at the age of 29, he was stabbed to death while in a pub in Deptford.

EXPLORERS AND EXPLORATIONS

William Adams was a trader and the first British navigator to reach Japan. Having sailed there, he heard that his wife back home had died, so he decided to make his home in Japan. Tragically, the news had been false, and his wife was very much alive. Adams took a Japanese wife, and it was only when she died that he returned to England, to find that his first wife was now also dead. He is much revered by the Japanese people for his advice on shipbuilding techniques, and many visit his statue in Gillingham.

THE ELIZABETHAN POOR LAW

The Elizabethan Poor Law was introduced in 1601 in an effort to bring relief to those who really needed it and to encourage those who did not to find gainful employment. Children were given apprenticeships, the able-bodied were set to work in a House of Industry, and those who were disabled or aged were looked after in almshouses. Those who did not fall into these categories but refused to work were sent to a House of Correction or even to prison.

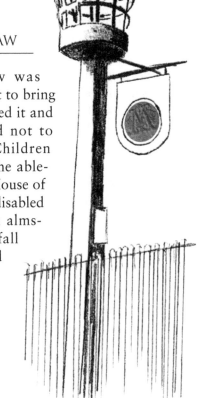

One of the millennium beacons, based on those installed to warn of the coming of the Spanish Armada

10

THE STUARTS

⚜ 1603–1714 ⚜

When Elizabeth I died, she had not named an heir, fearing that whoever was named might try to take the throne by force before her death. Of the several possible successors, the grandson of Elizabeth's cousin (James V), who was already James VI of Scotland, was considered the best choice and he came to the throne as James I of England. By 1600 the population of England had risen to just over 4 million, while the population of Kent stood at 150,000. The whole population, our Kentish family among them, were keen to see if James would follow Elizabeth's lead on the Church of England. He did, and he introduced more reforms such as the King James Bible, written in English. However, these reforms were controversial as they were not sweeping enough for some people, but a step too far for others and in 1605 a group of Roman Catholics tried to remove him from power by blowing up Parliament.

Dame Dorothy Selby of Ightham (pronounced 'Item') Mote may have saved the life of the king by warning her cousin Lord Mounteagle not to go to Parliament on 5 November. She had heard rumours that something was being planned, although she could not have known that Robert Catesby and his followers, including Guy Fawkes, were planning to blow up the king and Parliament that day, with barrels of gunpowder hidden in the cellars.

COMING TO ENGLAND ...

The British Empire had expanded, and noblemen from all corners of the globe were keen to visit England.

The Native American Algonquian princess we remember as Pocahontas married Englishman John Rolfe in 1614 and changed her name to Rebecca. A few years later, they came to London where she was accorded all the honours of a visiting ambassador. They were on their way home in the spring of 1617 when Pocahontas fell sick. She died at Gravesend aged 22 and is buried there, while her husband and son returned to America. Over time, her grave has been lost, but there is a statue of her in the graveyard, which was erected in 1958.

Her fate is echoed in that of Adela Wyman, daughter of an Englishman and an Inca princess who was taken ill in a visit to her father's birthplace in Littlebourne, near Canterbury, in 1862 and died two years later.

... AND LEAVING ENGLAND

Many people in England disliked both the Catholic and Anglican Churches and moved to the Netherlands to practise religion in the way they saw fit. Sadly, they were persecuted there as well and drew up plans to start a new life in the Americas, taking two ships, the *Speedwell* and the *Mayflower*.

One of the leaders of the *Mayflower* expedition, Robert Cushman, was born in Rolvenden and in 1620 he travelled to Canterbury to negotiate the hire of the *Mayflower*. He had originally planned to travel on the ill-fated *Speedwell*, which was unable to make the journey. He did travel to the New World in 1621, but stayed only two weeks and returned to become the agent of the Plymouth Colony in London.

In 1620, the *Mayflower* arrived in America after an arduous two-month voyage. Only one Kentish person was on board: Mary Chilton, who had been living in Leiden with her parents, had been baptised in Sandwich in 1607 and was 13 at the time of the voyage. Her father, James, was the oldest person at 64 years of age but he died on the voyage and was never to see the New World. Both Mary and her mother arrived safely in Massachusetts, though, and legend has it that Mary was the first person to set foot on Plymouth Rock. Sadly, her mother died shortly after arriving in America and Mary was adopted by another family. In 1623 Mary was given three shares of the land division, one for herself and one for each of her parents. She subsequently married, had ten children and lived until she was 70.

Charles I came to the throne in 1625 and later that year he travelled to Dover to meet his queen, Henrietta Maria, and escort her back to London. Charles returned to Kent in 1638 when he came on an official visit to the iron smelting works at Horsmonden to watch a cannon being cast. This was one of the largest iron works in Kent, and the Furnace Pond which provided water power for the plant is one of the largest artificial lakes in the country.

He was not a popular king, and the fact that his wife was a Roman Catholic was a worry to many people, although she was a welcome personality in some quarters and it was under her patronage that Tunbridge Wells became fashionable. Visitors had stayed at Tunbridge Wells since 1606 when the health of a courtier of James I had improved after he had sampled the spring water there, and the town grew in popularity.

AN AGE OF DISCOVERY

Kent is often remembered for being the birthplace of rebellion, but it has also grown its fair share of scientists.

William Harvey, for example, was born in Folkestone. He trained as a physician and in 1628 published *An anatomical study of the motion of the heart and of blood in animals* which described how the heart pumped blood around the body. The hospital at Ashford is named after him.

John Wallis of Ashford served as chief cryptographer for Parliament and is credited with introducing the symbol for infinity.

John Tradescant and his son worked in a different area of science and were both gardeners and botanists. John Tradescant the Younger was born in Meopham (pronounced 'Meppum') and was educated at The King's School, Canterbury. He travelled to America several times between 1628 and 1637, collecting specimens and making notes. Among the plants he introduced to English gardens are the magnolia, the lilac, phlox, asters and of course the house plant *Tradescantia*.

THE ENGLISH CIVIL WARS

At the beginning of the wars, it seemed that matters might be resolved relatively amicably, but many men in Kent felt that their point of view had to be voiced. In 1642, a petition to Parliament was drawn up calling for an end to the disagreements between the king and Parliament, and in particular the rescinding of the right of Parliament to control the militia. Copies were circulated around the country to be signed. Our Kentish family did not sign, as they were not in the voting class, but four boys from the family joined the group who went to present the petition, walking to Maidstone and prepared to fight for what they believed. Richard Lovelace delivered the petition but the signatories were arrested and a committee was set up in Maidstone to keep an eye on the Kentish rebels. The signatories were later ordered to appear in Parliament, after which they were arrested, although they were later bailed. Men were deciding which side to support and were testing the mettle of their opponents.

THE PLUM PUDDING RIOTS

By 1647 things has worsened and the Puritans issued an edict that Christmas should not be celebrated and that shops should open as usual on 25 December. The citizens of Canterbury ignored this and when the mayor stepped in, threatening to arrest the shopkeepers who refused to open, a riot ensued. Part rebellion, part Christmas celebrations and, weirdly, part street football, the rioting went on until the end of January when the ringleaders were arrested and put on trial at Maidstone. Luckily, they were released, and there were wild celebrations in Canterbury.

The men of the county had had enough and rose up against the Parliamentarian army, seeing in it a reflection of the hated County Committee. General Fairfax was sent with 3,000 men to quell the rabble of 7,000 which had gathered at Penenden Heath under the leadership of the Earl of Norwich. Unfortunately, when professional soldiers are pitted against angry rebels, the cool (round) heads of the soldiers triumphed, and by 1648 the Battle of Maidstone and the rebellion was over. A total of 300 men were killed and 1,000 arrested, although those from our Kentish family once more eluded capture and escaped back to their homes, along with many of their comrades. The Parliamentarians lost only eighty men.

Meanwhile, the Civil War rumbled on across the country and in 1649 the Mayor of Maidstone, Andrew Broughton, signed the death warrant of Charles I.

WITCH TRIALS

Witch trials were carried out at the beginning of the 1450s across England. Luckily, the men and women of Kent suffered far less than those in other counties. Four women were executed in Faversham for witchcraft, and five from Cranbrook. One from Lenham was hanged, but most of the witch trials in Kent ended in acquittals.

THE RESTORATION

In 1660 King Charles II landed at Dover to reclaim the throne. One of the men prominent in the organisation of the return was Samuel Pepys, who spent some time in Deal planning the event. He recorded his impressions in a diary, and these were not altogether complimentary. He was often rowed ashore to visit the pubs and taverns and was particularly fond of Margate ale. Pepys was one of the men who accompanied the king on his journey across Kent and into London, although the party of travellers grew as it progressed. Charles was greeted on Barham Downs by the county nobility and foot regiments of Kent, who escorted him to Canterbury and then to London via Rochester. The party stopped at Restoration House in Crow Lane, where the king was entertained on the night before the official restoration.

Restoration House, Rochester

WALLOONS AND HUGUENOTS

From 1661 to 1698 an estimated 50,000 Protestant Walloons and Huguenots fled to England from France, fleeing religious persecution. Not all of them stayed in Kent, but many gravitated towards Canterbury, where families were granted asylum. In 1681 the problems in France were so great that Charles II issued official sanctuary in this country and refugees were welcomed by the people of Kent. Services are still held in the Huguenot Chapel in Canterbury Cathedral in French every Sunday. Other evidence of the Walloons and Huguenots in Canterbury include a run of houses in Turnagain Lane where weavers' windows survive on the top floor, and the half-timbered house known as The Weavers. Rochester has a Huguenot museum and the French hospital there is an almshouse for the relief of their descendants.

As well as their skills in weaving, the Huguenots also brought with them their French style of cooking. The Crown Inn at Sarre is called Cherry Brandy House for the high-quality cherry brandy it serves, made from a secret Huguenot recipe.

SMUGGLING CONTINUES

The export of wool was made illegal in 1614 but smuggling wool out of England avoided the tax which had to be paid to the powerful guilds. The tax was an attempt to protect the interests of the guilds, which in turn paid tax to the Crown. The prevention of smuggling was in the hands of the riding officers, who were in effect freelance mounted policemen; their official title was The Land Service of Surveyors and Riding Officers. Along with the wool, smugglers exported grain, cannon and even guineas to pay French troops, all in exchange for luxury goods which were prohibitively expensive when bought through traditional channels. The post of riding officer carried on until 1865, despite the fact that many of the officers were paid to look the other way or were even more directly involved in the trade.

Shallow boats from Deal were used extensively by smugglers as they could outrun the larger customs vessels and be carried across the Goodwin Sands sandbanks at low tide, thus escaping capture. Some of the galleys, which were up to 40ft long, could hold as many as thirty oarsmen, and make the crossing to France in five hours.

THE GREAT PLAGUE

The Great Plague, which so affected London, also brought terror and heartache to more rural areas. Our Kentish family were accustomed to regular bouts of plague and knew that the royal family left the city to avoid plague season each year. In 1665, however, came a plague worse than any in living memory. Dover was badly hit, with an estimated 1,000 people dying during the year. The graveyards were unable to cope, and the local council of Dover bought a piece of land at Hougham (pronounced Huffam) between Dover and Folkestone, known locally as The Graves, to be used for the overflow bodies. Edward Hasted, the famed Kentish historian, reports that the dead were sometimes carried to the burial ground in coffins, but were more often just thrown into carts.

On a more positive note, Kentish bricks were in high demand after the Great Fire of London, as they were near enough to be sent up by barge. On the back of the wealth it brought, many thatched roofs in the county were replaced with Kent peg tiles. There was also a trend in this period for weather-tiling houses – that is, using wall-hung tiles to add an extra layer of protection to wattle-and-daub external walls. This was made possible by improvements in the tile industry, making tiles cheaper and more easily available.

MATTERS OF MEDWAY

Kent once again held its collective breath in June 1667 when, to the embarrassment of the British navy, the Dutch entered the Medway. They sailed up the Thames, looted Sheerness and broke through the chain barrier installed by Elizabeth I to get as far as Chatham. Upnor Castle proved to be ineffective and the intruders burnt ships and captured the *Royal Charles*. They landed at Sheppey to take supplies, but after making their point they were gone by the end of July. In response to this, Charles II ordered forts to be built at Gillingham and Cockham Wood.

HOP FIELDS ABOUND

From the 1670s hops started to be grown in greater numbers as corn prices fell; Kentish farmers had lots of chestnut trees, suitable for the practice of coppicing which encourages the trees to grow the long poles needed for the hop fields, and the forestry knowledge to grow them. Daniel Defoe estimated that there were 6,000 acres of hops being grown around Canterbury at the time he wrote his *Tour thro' the Whole Island of Great Britain*, but by the end of the nineteenth century this had grown to 77,000. Hops had been introduced to the county from the Netherlands some 100 years earlier, but had been used for fodder, green manure or even packing rather than in the flavouring of beer.

Shepherd Neame is one of the oldest brewers in Britain and still brews beer in Faversham. Named after Percy Beale Neame who amalgamated his family brewery with Shepherd and Mares brewery in 1877, it is one of the few breweries that are truly independent. Once, every town and almost every village and inn had its own brewery and the public house name 'tap' refers to the hotel it served – for instance, The Rose Tap served The Rose hotel or tavern.

Another of the larger Kent breweries was Fremlin's, who were taken over in 1967 by Whitbread. Surprisingly, the logo of the company features a large grey elephant, possibly a reference to its popular India Pale Ales. The Elephant pub at Faversham changed its name from The Two Brewers, to avoid confusion with a pub of the same name, and chose The Elephant as a nod to its premier supplier of beer.

THE GLORIOUS REVOLUTION

Our Kentish family were again troubled when James II succeeded his brother Charles II to the throne of England in 1685, as they were understandably suspicious of a monarch who followed the Roman Catholic Church and were fearful of a return to the persecutions of Mary Tudor's time. James had only reigned for three years when matters came to a head.

James' daughter Mary was a Protestant and had married the Dutch head of state William of Orange. They were backed by opponents of the king to take the throne from James, and another invasion through Kent seemed inevitable. However, William of Orange entered Britain from the west, avoiding Kent, and worked his way across country to London. By 1688, James had been deposed and William had become William II.

James escaped, but the ship in which he was travelling ran aground at Faversham. He was recognised, caught by fishermen and held prisoner until he could be transported back to London. He spent his last night on British soil at Abdication House in Rochester and then left from the Isle of Sheppey to join his family in France.

BEAU NASH

The discovery of the mineral spring in 1606 marked the beginning of Tunbridge Wells, and it forms a central part of Royal Tunbridge Wells today. Visitors came to see and be seen in fashionable Tunbridge Wells, but above all to 'take the waters'. The Walks, a paved area of square clay tiles, was laid in 1700 beside a row of colonnaded shops and was developed for the gentry; the lower classes were only allowed to use the lower walkways. We call this area The Pantiles.

Tunbridge Wells (which did not become Royal Tunbridge Wells until 1909) was a favourite haunt of Richard Nash, who was nicknamed Beau, and although popular, was considered to be somewhat less than respectable. He was a leader of fashion and appointed himself Master of Ceremonies in 1735, to the delight of his followers. His birthday is celebrated in October in Tunbridge each year.

The Pantiles, Royal Tunbridge Wells

THE TURNPIKE TRUST

By 1700 the atrocious state of the roads in Kent was causing concern, especially since the coach had been introduced as a method of transport in about 1650. Travel times were limited not by the type of transport chosen but by the condition of the roads to be travelled, these being much worse during the winter than in a dry summer period.

In 1709 the first turnpike road was opened under the governance of the Turnpike Trust, running from Sevenoaks through Tonbridge to Rye. Each stretch of road was the responsibility of a private entrepreneur who maintained the road in exchange for the toll revenue. Traffic was stopped by a gate, and the traveller would pay at the toll house before it was opened to allow access to the fully maintained roadway. These toll houses are visible today throughout Kent, and can be identified by the inward-opening windows with deep sills, adjacent to the road. The toll cottage at Nonington was an existing building pressed into service, but others were purpose-built, such as that at Chilham. The toll house at Whitstable lies at the junction of Joy Lane and Canterbury Road and due to modernisation of the traffic system has been left stranded on a central reservation.

THE GREAT STORM

The Great Storm of November 1703 was the worst storm on record until that of 1987, and almost ruined our Kentish family. Over 1,000 houses were destroyed in Kent and 1,200 lives were lost. The entire fleet of Sir Basil Beaumont was lost on the Goodwin Sands and in Whitstable a ship was blown 250yd inland.

Following this, plans were made for a more substantial harbour at Ramsgate, and work was started in 1749. The construction took almost 100 years to complete, and it is the only harbour in the UK which is allowed to call itself a royal harbour, a status later given by George IV who was much impressed with the hospitality he was offered by the townspeople.

DAILY LIFE

This was a period of decline for several of the staple industries that had brought wealth to the people of Kent. The iron industry deteriorated due to cheap imports and even the woollen industry moved further north. Kent fell back on the traditional industries of farming and agriculture. Times were harder and life in a typical village of the period can be guessed at from a visit to Chilham, which has a historic central square surrounded by many Tudor and Jacobean buildings. By the end of the Stuart period, our family were used to seeing more affluent families smoking tobacco and they had even tried a potato, although they were a little reticent to accept that either would ever come into general use.

The last Stuart monarch was Queen Anne, daughter of James II. She reigned for twelve years, but only visited the west of Kent, staying frequently at Lullingstone Castle.

11

THE HANOVERIANS

⇥ 1714–1837 ⇤

Although only fifty-second in line to the throne, George I of Hanover was chosen to succeed Anne for his Protestant beliefs. The rule of the House of Hanover is often called the Georgian period as three of the four monarchs were called George.

When George I arrived in Britain, he spoke only German, and his prime minister, Robert Walpole, assumed greater responsibility than any previous minister, sealing the relationship between monarch and prime minister for future generations. At the beginning of the Hanoverian period, the population of England stood at just over 5 million and did not stop growing, so that by the time Victoria came to the throne there were almost 8 million people in England.

Chatham Dockyard was further developed and the main gate of ornate brickwork was added in 1720; it stands to this day. The number of ships built at the dockyard was increased, and more than 100 ships were launched over the next century.

Kent continued as a primarily agricultural economy, which needed to be protected from rising prices, smuggling and the destruction of property. Our Kentish family were pleased to hear of the introduction of Acts of Parliament which would help to reduce the numbers of vermin on their land. This worked as a system of local clearance rewarded by payment via the Church; foxes, badgers, rats, sparrows, hedgehogs and even polecats were paid for. Even throughout the Victorian period and into the twentieth century, villages had Rat and Sparrow Clubs, whereby members would catch and record pests throughout the year and celebrate with an awards dinner at year's end. The boys in the family loved this, as they could wander the countryside together and earn a little money at the same time. At The Bull in Eastry, the 1913 count was 630 rats' tails and 973 sparrow heads, a not insignificant number considering that the other four pubs in the village were also collecting.

The British Empire expanded even further during the reign of George II, and the Kentish family were happy enough to learn the new tune *God Save the King* that had become popular. They were not so pleased about the changes to the calendar, when in 1752 the Gregorian calendar replaced the old Julian calendar, skipping eleven days and moving some Saints' Days to different dates. A good thing, though, in their opinion, was the moving of New Year's Day from 25 March to 1 January, extending the Christmas period. It is interesting to note that the modern tax year starts on 6 April, calculated to be eleven days from 25 March.

SEA BATHING

A new health remedy was introduced to the nation in 1736 when Thomas Barber advertised a salt-water bath at The New Inn in Margate, and Benjamin Beale invented the first bathing machine in 1753 whereby bathers went to a 'bathing room' (rather like a wooden caravan) which was pulled out into the sea by a horse. Once it was in position, the door could be opened so the bather could lower a set of steps and walk down into the water. Not only did this avoid the pebbles, but it also minimised the chance of anyone looking at their ankles. In 1791 John Coakley Lettsome opened his Sea Bathing Hospital in the town, which accepted patients until 1996, by then specialising in tuberculosis. Thalassotherapy, or treatment with seawater and seaweed, has now been recognised as a valuable homeopathic treatment.

ELEPHANTS IN THE LANDSCAPE

Elephants were supposedly brought to Chilham Castle to clear the newly redesigned grounds, but the Chilham Castle website is circumspect on the matter and says that contemporary documentation can neither prove nor disprove this story. It would be lovely to find out that it was true. A building on the edge of castle property considered to be the Elephant House is still visible from the main road, so perhaps it is.

GARRISONS AND GUNPOWDER

The only surviving Georgian fort in the Medway area is the Amherst Redoubt, which was constructed in about 1756 at the southern end of the Brompton lines of defence built to protect the south-eastern approaches to Chatham Dockyard and the River Medway against a French invasion. Fort Pitt and Fort Clarence were also erected in the area, which together with other forts were part of the defence works collectively called the Chatham Great Lines. These defences were put up in response to the Seven Years War, which began in 1756.

The series of fortifications and ditches from Rochester to Gillingham which comprised the Chatham lines were mirrored in the south by two artillery forts at Dover, which were linked by ditches.

A military camp was built at Coxheath and an army of 12,000 men was drawn together, mostly from Hesse and Hanover, in case reinforcements were needed in North America. The camp remained there until Canada was safely in British hands, closing in 1814. Similar camps were opened at Chatham, Barham and Shorncliffe.

The gunpowder works at Faversham was the town's main industry and the product was exported internationally, as well as to the nearby dockyards at Sheerness and Chatham and to the Tower of London. Today, the works, which were nationalised in 1759, are thought to be the oldest mills in the world, powered first with water and later with steam. The high demand for gunpowder during this period meant that works could be sustained at Dartford, Leigh and Tovil, alongside the Marsh, Oare and Home works at Faversham.

High-explosive production began in 1847, with several detonations rocking the local community; the largest was during the First World War, when 200 tons of explosive took over 100 lives. The mills were closed in 1934.

During the 1760s, an idea was mooted that a new road, avoiding Chatham city centre, should be created. The plan was approved, and in 1769 the first 'bypass' was built around Chatham. Happily, the road, built on higher ground with a view over the Medway, attracted housing investment and the town benefited.

As gun technology improved, the flints that were naturally abundant in the chalk hillsides and had been used during the Stone Age were again used when flintlock guns became widespread. The village of Chalk became renowned for the quality of its gun flints, which were in high demand both in England and abroad.

TWO KINDS OF VICTORY

In September 1759 the British attacked Quebec and took Canada from the French, which was widely celebrated as a significant victory for Britain. Sadly, the death of one British hero, General James Wolfe, soured the occasion and there was a period of national grief when people heard of the passing of this son of Kent. James was born in 1727 in Westerham vicarage and grew up in nearby Quebec House. He joined the army and first saw military action at the age of 16. After an illustrious career, culminating in the Battle of Quebec, James died at the age of 32, epitomising the British characteristics of heroism and courage in battle.

His senior officer was Jeffrey Amherst of Sevenoaks, who masterminded the attack and took Montreal the next year, securing the country as part of the British Empire. He was later knighted and died in Sevenoaks almost forty years later. He is widely remembered in Canada, with pubs and a town named after him, but in Kent, only one lonely obelisk reminds us of his heroic actions, along with the Napoleonic fort in Chatham that was named after him.

HMS *Victory* was built at Chatham Dockyard in 1765, taking six years to complete. However, it had a massive overhaul just before the Battle of Trafalgar, becoming Horatio Nelson's flagship in 1805.

Another notable fact of George III's reign was the start of the Industrial Revolution, with James Watt's famous steam engine bringing much misery to those whose jobs were lost. The gap between the rich and the poor increased considerably, and was brought to public notice by authors like Charles Dickens in his novels *David Copperfield* and *Oliver Twist*, amongst others.

WINDMILLS, WATERMILLS AND TIDE MILLS

Before the use of steam power became widespread, the industry of Kent was powered by wind- and watermills.

The Union Mill at Cranbrook, built in 1814, is the tallest surviving smock-style windmill in the British Isles and Herne Mill is also a Kentish smock mill, but dates from slightly earlier, having been built in 1789.

Originally at Farningham, the black weather-boarded windmill at West Kingsdown was actually moved in 1880. This was not that unusual, as millers tried mills in alternative positions. Interestingly, the Petham windmill was also moved to Stelling Minnis in 1840 – when the miller moved, he took the mill with him!

The mill at Haxted is a watermill, built in 1680, which has been restored and operates as a museum, and the tide mill at Deptford, powered by the incoming and outgoing tides, was changed to a steam-powered mill processing flour in the 1820s before it was demolished in the 1970s. Faversham Tidal Mill once operated on Faversham Creek, and the building is still visible from Standard Quay.

Cranbrook Mill, also known as Union Mill, is the tallest smock mill in the UK

THE FIRST CENSUS

The first national census since the Domesday survey was taken in 1801, collecting data on the number of houses and the number of people in a parish but with no individuals' details. The statistics showed that the population of Kent stood at just over 300,000 – double that at the end of Queen Elizabeth I's reign.

THE NAPOLEONIC WAR

Britain declared war on France in 1803 and the hearts of our Kentish family sank. They were once more going to be living on the front line under the constant threat of invasion. There was work to be had, though, and many members of the family were employed in the building industry, the manufacture of armaments and in ship-building at the shipyards on the north Kent coast.

It is a well-known local fact that Admiral Horatio Nelson stayed at the Royal Hotel in Deal with Lady Emma Hamilton. What is less well known is that it was a joint holiday with Lady Nelson, Sir William Hamilton and Horatio and Emma's daughter Horatia, who later married a vicar and raised her family in Kent.

At Dover, 3 miles of tunnels were built into the rock face leading up to the castle from the beach, as accommodation for the 2,000 troops stationed there (they were used during the wars of the twentieth century as well, both as air-raid shelters and as a military command centre) and the castle was strengthened with new artillery. Also at Dover was the Grand Shaft in the Western Heights cliffs, which is a triple staircase built to link the town with the barracks. The 140ft-deep shaft provided pedestrian access to the Western Heights fortress, in particular the Grand Shaft Barracks, from Snargate Street. It fell into disrepair until the 1990s, when it was refurbished.

Another major undertaking was that of the Royal Military Canal, which was constructed between Folkestone and Hastings to cut off any potential invading army, in the event that the French managed to get past the Royal Navy and the Martello towers. The plan was that cannon would be positioned along the canal at 400yd intervals, supported by soldiers and supplies which could be moved along the Military Road, which was protected by the bank of earth created when the canal was dug out. The canal runs for 28 miles, is 30ft wide and is recognised as an important tool in the irrigation of the marshes as well as being a haven for wildlife. Barges no longer travel along the canal, but it is possible to walk or cycle along the entire length.

Hundreds of local builders were given employment from 1805 onwards, as the county became home to the twenty-seven Martello towers erected between Folkestone and Dymchurch. These oval towers were three floors high, had an internal measurement of 13ft and were manned by about twenty-four men plus one officer. The Dymchurch Tower has been restored and visitors can see what conditions must have been like for the men as they waited for the attack. The ground floor of the tower was used as a storeroom, the first floor was the living quarters, and the top floor was the location of the 2.5-ton gun and two carronades.

Further along the coast is the Dymchurch Redoubt, the central one of three located in Essex, Kent and Sussex which acted as supply depots to nearby towers. Romney Marsh in particular was considered to be a potential landing spot for the French, and there were plans in place for the evacuation of residents should this happen.

There were also plans to remove or destroy crops and cattle to keep them from falling into enemy hands.

THE GUNPOWDER WORKS AT LEIGH

As war with France threatened, enterprising men of Kent realised that there was money to be made in gunpowder, and a gunpowder works was set up at Leigh in the early 1800s. One of the main ingredients, charcoal, was sourced locally, but 90 per cent of the materials would have been imported and brought up the River Medway by ship or barge. The works grew fast and provided employment for hundreds of local people, many of whom lived in workers' cottages near the plant, separate from the main village. It closed in 1934, when ICI, which by then owned the site, moved operations elsewhere. Gradually the site was completely dismantled and it has only recently received archaeological interest.

KENT ASYLUMS

Our extended Kentish family looked after two people: an elderly relative with dementia and an older boy with Down's Syndrome, who might both have been taken to the 'madhouse' if they had not been cared for at home. Before the 1774 Madhouse Act, unlicensed practitioners ran homes for those mentally ill patients who could no longer be looked after at home, and with no governing body, the homes were often very poorly run and were used as a last resort by those who could not look after their relatives themselves. The Madhouse Act ensured that each house was licensed and subject to an annual inspection.

Things gradually improved, and in 1808 the County Asylum Act was passed, which encouraged the building of county asylums along with the right to collect taxes in order to fund the venture. In places where no independent madhouse had been set up, mentally ill parishioners had often been left in workhouses, so the new asylums provided dedicated care and nursing, restoring some of their dignity as bona fide patients.

SMUGGLING BECOMES BIG BUSINESS

After the Napoleonic War, the government needed to refill the coffers and decided to do this by raising taxes, so it introduced taxes on sprits, tobacco, linen and tea. This did not go down well with our Kentish family, and the young men of many local families decided to do something about it. The smuggling that had always been prevalent along the coast, particularly on the sparsely populated marshes, began to grow into something much more dangerous.

Much has been written about the Kentish smugglers, and histories vary in their reports, but the largest gangs – the Hawkhurst Gang, the North Kent Gang, the Aldington Gang and the Groombridge Gang – were reputed to have as many as 500 members, although these would not all be working at the same time. One or two of the younger members of our Kentish family joined, as they could earn more in one night's smuggling than from a week's normal work. They smuggled tobacco, spirits, tea and lace. During the day they would follow their usual trade and at night might be asked to act as a lookout, to distract the Revenue Men, to ferry goods to waiting ships or to pass imported goods on to the customers. Smugglers avoided both customs duty paid on items coming into the country and excise duty paid on goods leaving. By 1809 it was estimated that there were over 20,000 smugglers operating along the Kent/Sussex coast.

Between 1793 and 1814 vast numbers of prisoners of war were brought to England, many kept in appalling conditions on the prison ship hulks in the Thames and Medway. During this time, Kentish smugglers helped them to get home, for a fee from their family.

In 1816 the system of riding officers and coastguards was reinforced with the Coastal Blockade, and officers were either given purpose-built cottages or housed in the obsolete Martello towers. By 1820 it comprised 6,708 officers and men, including 2,375 men on thirty-one Royal Navy ships, and the service stayed active until 1831.

TRAVEL AND TOURISM

In the 1820s the tourist trade started to develop as people once again felt that it was safe to visit the south coast. Dover developed Waterloo Crescent and Marine Parade, and Folkestone also developed a curving row of stone-clad houses in Marine Parade, styled after The Crescent at Bath, and began its change from sleepy fishing village into trendy travel destination. Gravesend became particularly popular due to its proximity to London and in Margate two new squares were built. The seaside holiday had arrived!

Fortunately for travellers, it was at about this time that Macadam's idea of paving the roads with hard, rolled stone was introduced, and the poor and unemployed were put to work finding and chipping stones to be used on the highways.

The first paddle steamship on the Thames arrived at Margate in 1815, travelling on to Ramsgate, which was the end of the line. This gave Margate the boost it needed and its annual visitor numbers rose from less than 20,000 to 135,000 over the next twenty years. Each of the towns needed a pier at which the steamer could dock, and these blossomed into the pleasure piers which became an integral part of the seaside experience. Herne Bay's pier was built in 1832, Gravesend's in 1834, Sheerness's in 1835 and Deal's in 1838. All these were updated from wooden to ironwork construction in the second half of the nineteenth century.

In 1796, the system of beacons instigated by Elizabeth I was improved and became a system of semaphore or 'shutter telegraph' stations. Using this system, a message could travel from the coast to London in a matter of minutes. Stations were installed at Shooter's Hill, Swanscombe, Gad's Hill, Beacon Hill, Shottenden Hill, Barham Downs, Betteshanger and Deal. The tower at Deal was adapted in 1855 to become a timeball tower, whereby a ball is raised and lowered at set times as an aid to those offshore.

THAMES AND MEDWAY CANAL

Thames and Medway Canal opened in 1824 and ran for 7 miles between Gravesend and Strood, saving barges a 47-mile trip around the Isle of Grain from Gravesend to Strood, and it included a 2-mile-long tunnel between Strood and Higham. When the railways came to prominence, train tracks were laid along the towpath and in 1847 the canal was bought by the South Eastern Railway, which emptied it and laid tracks along its length. The Strood end has been filled in so that the land can be used for housing.

LIFESAVING AND LIFEBOATS

Purpose-built lifeboats appeared in Kent from about 1800, although they had been invented in 1785. Some were privately owned, but they were eventually taken over by the Royal National Lifeboat Institution (RNLI) when it was formed in 1824. In 1881 the Ramsgate boat *Bradford* was successful in saving the crew of the *Indian Chief,* and this became the most notable rescue ever carried out by a British lifeboat.

DAILY LIFE

Machines that had been introduced onto the land during the Napoleonic War, when labour was scarce, were now used throughout the county, taking the jobs of farm labourers and their families.

In 1823, William Cobbett rode through Kent and noted that although agriculture seemed to be thriving, the poor of the county were exceptionally beggarly, in his opinion more so than those of neighbouring counties. By the 1830s there were famine conditions in the county, and half the parishes in Kent were giving relief to families with more than three children, our Kentish family among them. Families which relied upon poor relief for 15 per cent or more of their income were classified as paupers, and this accounted for almost half the labourers in Kent.

This seems an appropriate time to point out that the sandwich as an item of food has very little to do with the town of Sandwich. In 1762, the 4th Earl of Sandwich did ask for meat between two slices of bread to be served to him at the gambling table, but his title was purely honorary. The 1st Earl of Sandwich almost took the title Earl of Portsmouth, and if this had been the case, things would have turned out very differently.

THE SWING RIOTS

The economic depression following the Napoleonic War was exacerbated by bad harvests and was felt keenly in Kent. In 1830, labourers started an uprising by smashing threshing machines at Hardres, a village near Canterbury. The rioting spread throughout the Elham Valley and further afield to Dover, and by the third week over 100 machines had been destroyed. To underpin the reasons for the unrest, farmers received threatening letters signed 'Captain Swing', but historians cannot agree on whether this was one person, or a title attributed to the movement. Some of the rebels were caught and tried at the East Kent sessions, and many escaped with light sentences. However, of the 102 who were tried in different courts, four were executed, forty-eight imprisoned and fifty-two transported. Many people were sympathetic to the labourers, and understood their plight. The Poor Law Amendment Act of 1834 was designed to alleviate the problem, but encouraged the building of workhouses, which were anything but popular.

KENT WORKHOUSES

Previous to the 1834 Act, each parish had decided on the best way to deal with its poor, but after 1834 the responsibility passed to the newly formed Poor Law Unions. Each union was under the guidance of a Board of Guardians, much like schools today are overseen by school governors, but they did not have a role in the day-to-day running of the institutions.

The guardians appointed staff, including a medical officer and a relieving officer, to whom those in need would apply in the first instance. Each union had its own workhouse, which might cover several parishes, and could offer 'indoor' relief if it was deemed necessary. All types of people came for aid, including the insane, the sick and the elderly. Once admitted to the workhouse, men and women were separated. Kent had a number of sister institutions that could be used to take certain patients, and those in need, once assessed, might be sent to a lunatic asylum, hospital, children's home or training home.

Some people suffering from the agricultural depression and were offered 'outdoor' relief, which might be a payment towards their rent, food, clothing, school fees, payment of a marriage licence or even a ticket to the New World.

The unions provided help until 1929 when county councils took over the responsibility, but several independent organisations such as the Ramsgate Sailor's Church (1878) and the Smack Boys Home (a smack was a type of boat) (1881) continued to provide extra relief.

George IV died in 1830, and was succeeded by his brother, William IV, in 1831.

CRICKET

The Vine at Sevenoaks is said to be the oldest cricket ground in England, although many others also lay claim to the title. The Vine was given to the town of Sevenoaks in 1773 by the owner of Knole House, the Duke of Dorset, after the first reported cricket match had already been played there in 1734, at which Kent defeated Sussex.

INDUSTRY

In 1834, William Aspdin began to make Portland cement at Northfleet, which was thought to resemble the popular building material Portland stone. He made use of the local deposits of chalk and clay as raw materials and used the Thames as a convenient method of transportation for the finished product. The cement industry grew and, although it employed hundreds of people, it has left deep scars on the landscape; Aspdin's patent kiln is now a listed monument.

Kent, like Essex, is lucky to have the golden highway of the Thames to transport its crops and manufactured goods into London. The Thames barge was developed with a flat bottom to enable it to navigate the narrow creeks and inlets of these counties, and yet still be able to cope with high tides on the Thames Estuary. The very first barges lacked the large red sails which we associate so readily with the Thames barge, but these quickly developed to catch and tame the winds more efficiently. By the early twentieth century, 200 Thames barges were registered, which were of various sizes, from 100 to 300 tonnes.

Even as late as the 1930s, sailing barges brought refuse from London to the north Kent brickyards, providing rich pickings for anyone brave enough to rake through, seeking discarded jewellery or coins. Dubbed the 'rough stuff', the piles were left for a year for any vegetable matter to rot, before they were burnt for use in the brickmaking process. The yellow London stock brick required 64 per cent brick earth, 25 per cent ash and 11 per cent chalk.

Villages on the north Kent coast like Pluckley, Rainham, Pembury and Hoo were all brick-producing areas, along with Dunton Green, which produced particularly high-quality bricks. The Dunton Green Brick, Tile and Pottery Works, which was established in 1862 using the local gault clay, invested in the first mechanical brick-making machine in England, and continued production until the clay deposits were exhausted in the mid-1950s.

The Canterbury tanning industry was started in 1790 by Stephen Williamson, who first opened a shop in the town centre before setting up a tannery in the town. During the Napoleonic War, there were 5,000 troops stationed in the area who all needed boots, harnesses and other leather items. Despite complaints about the stink of the tannery processes so close to the city centre, the business grew and expanded. The high-quality leather was later used as car upholstery in luxury car brands, but demand dropped and the site closed in the late twentieth century. Dover, Ashford and Cranbrook all had tanneries processing hides with the oak bark from Wealden forests.

LIFE IMPROVES

Once the economic depression that followed the Napoleonic War had lifted, and the daily threat of starvation was gone, things improved. The next fifty years turned out to be a good time for those in the farming industry, and our Kentish family had amassed a little land over the years, working their way up from smallholders to landowners, albeit on a small scale. Even though imported American wheat lowered local prices, fruit and hops were still a profitable choice for the farmer, as were less common commodities such as watercress, lavender and mint. The family's small-scale farm was a huge benefit towards the end of the century, when cheap imports further lowered crop prices. They were able to experiment with new procedures and weather the storm with little fall in profits.

In 1837, William IV died and the throne passed to his 18-year-old niece Victoria, who ruled until 1901.

A Thames barge in full sail

12

THE VICTORIANS

⚜ 1837–1901 ⚜

The reign of Queen Victoria was dominated by the expansion of the British Empire, which spread to all five continents, from Canada and the Caribbean to Australia and New Zealand, including Africa, India and South-East Asia. By the time she died, Victoria ruled 40 per cent of the globe, which comprised 25 per cent of the world's population.

The period also saw a rapid rise in the population of the home nations; at the beginning of her reign there were only 13 million people in England, but by the end there were over 30 million, 500,000 of whom lived in Kent.

PRINCESS VICTORIA IN KENT

Before she became queen, the young Princess Victoria visited Kent regularly, staying in both Ramsgate and Tunbridge Wells. She first came to Ramsgate in 1823 at the age of 4 with her mother, the Duchess of Kent, and they stayed at Townley House in Chatham Street where she was allowed to play with the other children and have donkey rides on the beach. She also spent some time at Albion House and West Cliff House in Ramsgate.

Tunbridge Wells got its royal prefix from Victoria and her family, the Duke and Duchess of Kent, and it is thought that the first time she took a train ride was to visit her aunt in Tunbridge Wells at Calverley House. Victoria last visited the house in 1835.

CHILD LABOUR

An agricultural labourer earnt about 9s 6d per day, which was, surprisingly, less than they would have earnt had they lived in the northern counties. An average annual wage in Kent was about £25 per year, whereas the average for all counties was £31; a general labourer was worth slightly more, by about 5s per week.

These incomes were supplemented by the work of the wives and children, for although a woman had housework to do, and was almost always pregnant or nursing, she also undertook a variety of fieldwork, especially at busy times. In hopping season, the whole family would remove to the hop fields for the day, eating their dinner outside and not returning home until the light faded.

A child who worked as an agricultural labourer would work from 7 a.m. until 6 p.m. The work included stone picking, weeding, bird scaring or light field work such as planting. The stones picked from the fields were used to mend the roads.

HOPPING

Ripe hops, suspended on long chestnut poles coppiced in the local woodland, and strung by hand each spring, needed to be picked in September. This was labour-intensive work and every acre needed about 2,000 pickers to work for just under a month. Local labourers were already employed in their year-round jobs, so farmers looked to London where they found a band of labourers willing to live on site and work as a family for the period of the harvest. As hop season was followed by apple and plum season, many went on to pick the fruit crops on neighbouring farms before returning home.

A traditional Kentish oast house with its iconic revolving cowl

At first, the hoppers came 'on spec' and walked to the nearest farm to ask for work. A hundred years later, they were required to register at an agent in London before travelling down in buses, vans or by rail with all they needed for the time they were there. In particularly busy seasons the railway companies put on extra trains called 'hoppers' specials', and by the end of the century, these trains were carrying up to 20,000 hoppers into the Kentish countryside each year.

The first conical oast house, so iconic of the Kentish countryside, was developed by John Read in 1835, and it took over from the square or rectangular designs previously in use. The white cowls dominated the landscape as wind- and watermills had done previously, each turned by a windvane and more often than not mounted with a weathervane.

BATTLE OF BOSSENDEN WOOD

The Battle of Bossenden Wood took place in May 1838 near Hernhill in Kent and has been called the last battle on English soil. The battle was fought by a small group of labourers from the Hernhill, Dunkirk and Boughton area against a detachment of over 100 soldiers from the 45th Regiment of Foot. The self-styled Sir William Courtenay, who was actually John Nichols Tom, from Cornwall, had spent four years in Kent County Lunatic Asylum and declared himself to be Christ returned. In the days that led up to the battle, a growing number of people had engaged in boisterous but not riotous behaviour, gathering force as they went. A constable, Nicholas Mears, and his brother were sent to arrest Courtenay, and died in the attempt, after which events quickly escalated and the military was sent in. Eleven men lost their lives in the brief confrontation: Courtenay, eight of his followers and two of those sent to apprehend them. At the assizes which followed, Courtenay's followers were discharged as it was deemed they had been 'led astray' by Courtenay.

Soon afterwards, Dunkirk church was built to rectify what was seen as a lack of moral guidance from the Church.

BUFFS AND PIPPINS, FUGGLES AND FILBERTS

Our Kentish family had enjoyed wild hazelnuts for centuries, and seen gardens filled with cultivated varieties from the sixteenth century. The Kentish cob nut was introduced around 1830 and growers took advantage of the London market to promote their product. By 1913, 7,000 acres of farmland had been planted with cobnuts, in orchards called 'plats', most of which were in Kent. The longer, more oval-shaped nuts are known as filberts.

Victorians were passionately fond of farm stock competitions and in 1886 the Black Orpington chicken was bred by William Cook to produce high-quality eggs and meat, rather than one or the other. Cook selected a black bird primarily so that it would exhibit well by hiding the dirt and soot of London, and he also created the Buff Orpington which is famous throughout the world for its egg-laying capacity and fluffy good looks.

On the farm, George Bunyard and his sons developed several varieties of apple at Penenden Heath, including the Maidstone Favourite and the eternally popular

Allington Pippin, which can be used for both cooking and eating.

The rise of the best-known hop varieties lies somewhat shrouded in the mists of time. The Golding Hop had been grown since about 1760, and by the mid-1800s had developed into the Fuggle's Golding, which was so much better that by 1950 it made up almost 80 per cent of the British hop harvest. The Fuggle hop variety is said to have been a natural mutant that was spotted and developed by Mr Fuggle, although *which* Mr Fuggle is a matter of some debate.

In horticulture, Edward Banks of Sholden was one of the country's leading fuchsia growers, introducing varieties such as Beauty of Sholden. His cultivar forget-me-not appeared on the badge of the British Fuchsia Society in 1963.

LIGHTHOUSES

The coastline around Kent is notoriously dangerous for shipping, from the shallow shingle of Dungeness, past the Goodwin Sands, round the perilous edge of Thanet where the Thames meets the North Sea, and on to London, passing the Nore sandbank. The Romans were the first to install lighthouses to guide ships into the estuary at Dover, and they have been a necessary part of keeping ships and sailors safe ever since.

The first North Foreland Lighthouse at Kingsgate was erected in 1636 and the current one operated between 1843 and 1988, as a sister to the South Foreland Lighthouse, warning shipping about the Goodwin Sands. Many changes have taken place and the beacon, once an open fire, is now powered by electricity.

The South Foreland Lighthouse was also installed to warn ships about the treacherous Goodwin Sands, helping ships to navigate towards Dover. Prior to 1904, there had been two lighthouses on the site, which navigators would line up to gauge their passage. In the 1860s, Michael Faraday spent time at the lighthouse and, as a consequence, it was the first lighthouse to use electric light. In 1898 the first ship-to-shore radio transmission was successfully undertaken, which was quickly followed by communication with operatives at Boulogne. The lighthouse was decommissioned in 1989.

The shoreline at Dungeness was a further hazard to shipping, with the ever-increasing longshore drift causing problems. The first lighthouse was made of wood and had been installed in 1615, but was replaced by a brick one in 1625. The problems of the build-up of shingle necessitated the building of a new lighthouse in 1901, which operated until the current power station masked it from view, rendering it useless.

RAILWAYS

The coming of the railways revolutionised life in Kent. Fresh produce could reach the lucrative London market more quickly, travel was easier and the trains brought thousands of tourists to the county who might otherwise have gone straight past Kent on their way to the continent.

The earliest railway in Kent was the Canterbury to Whitstable Railway, which opened in 1830. It had been built by George Stephenson and carried the first passenger train in the country along its tracks, powered by a steam locomotive named *Invicta*, built in the style of Stephenson's more famous *Rocket*. Unfortunately, the gradient proved too much for its 12-horsepower engine, and for most of the journey the carriages were hauled along by cables attached to two steam-driven engines, one at the Winding Pond in Clowes Wood and the other at The Halt on Tyler Hill Road. The line was a pioneer in railway design, using such cutting-edge techniques as embankments, cuttings, level crossings, bridges and a tunnel. The journey took 40 minutes and the gates of the old 'Crab and Winkle Line', as it came to be known, remain at Whitstable Harbour spanning the entrance to the harbour opposite the Gorrell Tank reservoir, proudly showing the South Eastern and Chatham Railway logo.

The first South Eastern Railway line was laid in 1842–3 and by the 1850s the network had expanded to Ashford, Ramsgate, Canterbury, Tunbridge Wells and the Medway towns. Trains arrived in London at London Bridge, Charing Cross or Cannon Street and came to Dover in 1844, which supported the passage of continental travellers to the Great Exhibition in London in 1851. For the first time, our Kentish family and their friends could travel to the coast for a day out. The railways, which had at first been installed to carry freight, were adapted for carrying passengers across the county and beyond.

The London, Chatham and Dover Railway also operated in Kent, arriving in London at Victoria or Blackfriars. The two lines vied for business and it is because of this that villages like Chartham have two railways passing within a third of a mile of each other, as the companies bid for the right to build the local station. The two companies merged in 1899, forming the South

Eastern and Chatham Railway, and then further amalgamated with other railways under the Railways Act 1921 to form the Southern Railway.

The *Orient Express* started to pass through Kent from 1883, with travellers going by train from London Victoria to Dover, by steamer to Calais and then on to Paris by train. The service continued until 1936, by which time the sleeping carriages actually went on the ferry, but the service lost favour after the war. The story did not end there, however, as a luxury service to Venice was resumed in 1982 using 1920s and 1930s carriages. Once a year special trains run from London to Istanbul and the Kentish family love to see it pass their home, using modern tracks but exuding a pre-war charm.

Today, Kent has more open railway crossings on lesser-used footpath routes than any other county, including the one near Coldblow Farm just south of Deal, where drivers have to stop their car and open the wooden gates either side of the tracks themselves before they can pass, reclosing the gates afterwards. Despite this, there are no more accidents than in any other county.

WIND POWER

Much is spoken about the new windfarms on the Kentish Flats, but the Kentish economy has been powered by windmills for centuries. As the Industrial Revolution began to build, mills were pressed into greater and greater use before being replaced by steam engines.

Drapers Windmill, Margate, is a Kentish smock mill built in 1845 by master millwright John Holman of Canterbury. Bidborough Mill is a tower mill, probably built in about 1858. The Chillenden Mill has been extensively restored, and is one of the few post mills in Kent. Willesborough Windmill is one of the largest smock mills in the south of England, built in 1869 and remaining a working mill until the 1950s. Many other windmills have been renovated and function as museums which can be visited by the public, eight owned and operated by Kent County Council, and several under private ownership. The White Mill at Sandwich has been extended to include a Rural Heritage Centre.

THE CRIMEAN WAR

In 1854, the United Kingdom was brought into the Crimean War, supporting the Ottoman Empire against Russia. Coincidentally, this was the same year children were offered a smallpox vaccine, which was the start of world eradication of the disease, finally achieved in 1980. One of the best-known figures of the Crimean War was Florence Nightingale, who pioneered modern nursing. When she returned to England, Fort Pitt, between Rochester and Chatham, became the home of the first Florence Nightingale Army Medical School. What had begun as an ordinary military hospital in 1803, then had become part of the protection for the Royal Naval Dockyard at Chatham and later a hospital for invalided soldiers, was to be the birthplace for some of the nursing techniques we use today. The hospital closed in 1919.

Visitors can admire the huge brass gates in the Crimean Memorial Arch at the Brompton Barracks, Chatham, made from the Russian guns taken at Sebastopol. The gates were erected in 1860 in memory of the men of the Royal Engineers who fell during the campaign.

KENT CONSTABULARY

An Act of Parliament was passed in 1857 which required every borough and county to set up a local police force. Until this date, the local police officers interpreted the law according to the ideas of the district landowners or magistrates. As travel between towns and villages become increasingly easy, so crime increased and more constables were needed. It was assumed at first that these would be largely illiterate, although those employed as officers were required to be able to read and write. After three months' training at Maidstone, 220 constables were issued with a pocket guide and a uniform and put to work. Today, the force has 6,100 staff, juggling responsibilities at both national and international level, with one of the busiest road networks in the country, three ports and the Channel Tunnel all under their jurisdiction.

At one time, convicted felons in the Medway area were sent to Chatham Prison, which was built to house serious offenders and operated between 1854 and 1893. Prior to this, prisoners were housed in the prison hulks moored along the Medway, which had once been used to imprison Napoleonic prisoners of war. The prison, which was a 'hard labour' establishment, supplied a workforce for the building of the Chatham dockyards. The county currently has seven prisons.

CRICKET

Ye Olde Beverlie pub in Canterbury has a very early association with the game of cricket, said by some to be derived from the pub game Bat and Trap, and it was the home to the original Beverley Cricket Club before it transferred to the St Lawrence cricket ground. The earliest games were played on Beverley Meadow, and Canterbury Cricket Week originated here. It was on this village green that the first ever game of cricket in England was played.

Kent County Cricket Club was formed in 1859 at Maidstone. John Wilkes from Sutton Valance is credited with the introduction of round-arm bowling, which, after several 'no-ball' decisions, was eventually adopted throughout the sport.

A local tradition is the practice of playing cricket on the Goodwin Sands. Well known amongst sailors for the centuries of shipwrecks which have occurred there, the area has gained notoriety as 'Calamity Corner'. The first recorded cricket match on the sands was in 1824, organised by Ramsgate harbour master Captain K. Martin. Players arrive at the sands by boat just before low tide and wait for the first moment they can step onto dry(ish) land. They then have less than an hour to play before sailing back to the mainland.

FORTS AND FORTIFICATIONS

Fort Borstal was built using convict labour between the years of 1875 and 1885, following the 1859 Royal Commission on the Defence of the United Kingdom, to hold the high ground south-west of Rochester in the event of an invasion by the French.

Fort Burgoyne, originally called Castle Hill Fort, was built as one of the Palmerston Forts around Dover in south-east England. The Palmerston Forts were also built in response to the Royal Commission and were part of the largest maritime defence programme since Henry VIII had built his device forts.

Cliffe Fort is a disused artillery fort built in the 1860s to guard the entrance to the Thames from sea-borne attack and was also one of the Palmerston Forts, while Slough Fort (1867) is a small artillery fort that was built at Allhallows-on-Sea in the north of the Hoo Peninsula, intended to guard a vulnerable stretch of the River Thames.

PAPERMAKING

In 1861 the excise duty on paper was abolished and paper mills expanded their production across Kent, whose abundance of both water and trees made it an ideal papermaking landscape. As the price of raw materials fell and interest in magazines and newspapers increased, so did the demand for paper, and mills were built at Dartford, Northfleet, Sittingbourne and New Hythe. When there was not enough local wood available, wood pulp was imported from the Baltic or Canada. One of the raw materials brought in was the rags that formed the basis of high-quality writing paper. This was shipped from London by barge and processed in the Maidstone mills where the water was low in minerals.

The paper mill at Chartham was erected in the early 1700s and grew in size, working throughout the Victorian period. By the middle of the twentieth century the mill was producing a quarter of the world's tracing paper, which is still a speciality.

The Roughway Paper Mill at Plaxtol opened in 1807 and was in operation until the 1930s. It is said that the local people 'liberated' small quantities of the blue dye used at the factory to mix with their whitewash, giving the interiors of their cottages a distinctive local colour.

Mills in the Len and Loose Valleys that had previously been used for fulling were updated so they could process paper instead of cloth. Mills on the Stour, the Dour and the Darent were similarly co-opted.

BOAT BUILDING

Boat, barge and shipbuilding have been giving employment to generations of men from Kent – from Chatham and Sheerness to Faversham and Whitstable, from Deal and Dover to Romney and Hythe – for generations. Boats were needed for trade, fishing, travel and for the defence of the kingdom, and were paid for by private enterprise or by the Crown. One reminder of the fishing industry is the Smoke Hole or Herring Hang on Dungeness beach, which has been in operation since the early 1800s; another is the popularity of the Dover sole, which has become highly regarded worldwide.

The village of Conyer has been occupied since Roman times and was a centre of the barge-building industry on the north coast, constructing the barges that plied to and from London, bringing raw materials and returning finished goods. One of the materials they brought down was the cinders from household fires which were used in the production of bricks. The boat-building trade flourished throughout the nineteenth century, up until 1914, when the last boat was launched. Over this period it is believed that the men at Conyer built over 500 barges.

Whitstable, too, had several boat-building yards creating and maintaining the fishing fleet of oyster yawls that worked off its coast. Alongside this industry, the skills of the sail-maker, leather-worker, rope-maker and iron-worker all prospered. Over 130 vessels were built in Whitstable from 1775 onwards. Although the Thames barges mostly kept to the Thames Estuary and along the nearby coast, ships for trading further afield were also built here, travelling as far as the Azores for bananas, Alicante for citrus fruit, and round the Mediterranean to Greece and North Africa for other cargos. Another oft-forgotten business was the ice trade; ships would travel to Scandinavia to bring back ice for commercial and private use.

EDUCATION

The Education Act was passed in 1870, after which all children between the ages of 5 and 10 were required to attend school on a daily basis, it being the parents' duty to ensure that they attended. Previously, the only schooling many children received had been from the Sunday Schools, which were run by churches for the benefit of the poor. Unlike in modern Sunday Schools, pupils were offered up to eight hours of tuition and stayed at school for the whole day. At the beginning of Victoria's reign, only eleven elementary schools had existed in Kent, run by independent trusts. With their business concerns expanding, the children of our Kentish family had all been taught to read and write and were well versed in functional mathematics, even if algebra and geometry were unknown to them. All they needed was enough knowledge to count a consignment or payment and to be able to read an invoice or contract.

A few pennies a week was charged for the schooling, although this was waived for the poorest families. The agreed fees were often on a sliding scale, such as 3*d* for the first child, 2*d* for the second and 1*d* for the third and subsequent children. Children who lived locally went home for dinner at what we call lunchtime, while those who travelled some distance were allowed to bring dinner with them.

The year 1891 saw the abolition of the 'school penny', which was the fee for attending school, after which date the school claimed 10*s* per child per year from the county. School leaving age was raised to 11 in 1893 and to 12 in 1899, which had a serious impact on those in our Kentish family who relied on the earnings of their children to make ends meet. However, many of the neighbours' children did not attend school at all for this reason.

ELEPHANTS IN MARGATE

In 1870s the tearoom that had become famous as The Hall by the Sea was bought by George Sanger and renamed Dreamland. He kept, among other things, lions, tigers and elephants at the site for the entertainment of the crowds, before selling the venue in 1905.

ARTISTS IN KENT

The artist Van Gogh stayed in Ramsgate for three months in 1876, working as a teacher for board and lodging only. All that survives of the work he did while he was staying there are two drawings of Royal Road, on the seafront.

Just after this, William L. Wyllie moved to Hoo St Werburgh and lived there for twenty years from 1887. He is famous for his marine paintings in both oil and water-colour, which today sell for tens of thousands of pounds.

KENT ASYLUMS

It was not until the passing of the County Asylum Act in 1845 that widespread construction of asylums began to take place as counties were then legally obliged to provide asylums for their 'lunatics'.

Asylums in Kent were built at Darenth Park, Dartford (1878), Oakwood, Maidstone (originally the Kent County Asylum) (1833), St Augustine's, Chartham (originally the Kent County Asylum) (1885), St Martin's, Canterbury (originally Canterbury Borough Asylum) (1902) and Stone House, Dartford (1866). Only St Martin's is still open.

THE HEADQUARTERS OF IMPERIAL FRANCE

After the defeat of Napoleon III in 1879, he and his family moved to Kent, and set up the Headquarters of Imperial France at Camden Place in Chislehurst. Queen Victoria visited several times, to the delight of the local residents. Napoleon III and his son Prince Louis Napoleon were both buried in the family mausoleum at Chislehurst before being moved to Farnborough in 1892.

FOLKESTONE'S CLIFF LIFT

Our Kentish family were grateful that wherever they moved to within Kent, they were always within reach of the sea. Folkestone's Victoria Pier was opened in July 1888, and was initially a popular tourist destination. However, visitor numbers declined in the twentieth century and after the middle of the pier was deliberately bombed in 1940 as part of the defence system it never recovered its former glory. It fell into disrepair and the remains were eventually taken down in the 1950s.

The Leas Lift funicular railway was opened in 1885 to carry visitors from the top of the cliffs to the water's edge just at the entrance to the Victoria Pier. The twin lift cars on the railway are raised and lowered as water is pumped from one side to the other, thus exchanging the weight difference. It is undergoing restoration work at the time of writing.

THE BOER WARS

Several Kentish regiments were involved in the Second Boer War (1899–1902) during which Britain engaged with the Dutch-speaking settlers of South Africa, and in 1904 a monument was unveiled in Dane John Gardens, Canterbury, to honour the 300 Kent soldiers who lost their lives during the campaign.

EXTRAORDINARY WEATHER

The last quarter of the nineteenth century was witness to a range of extreme weather conditions, including drought, flood, ice and tidal waves.

In November 1877 a series of tidal waves struck the north Kent coast, causing damage to vessels on and off the shore.

This was followed in 1881 by more extraordinary weather. A blizzard in January brought with it a hurricane-force wind, wreaking havoc on the Kent coast. The promenade at Folkestone was washed away, and a train at Ramsgate was buried under 16ft of snow. Post Office telegraphs were suspended, as were the mail trains, and at Woolwich twenty-six barges were lost. Our Kentish family were unable to work their land during the freeze and had a hard task before them when the weather broke and meltwater flooded the fields.

The next year, they and their neighbours were amazed to see the aurora borealis which was visible in 1882. The local newspaper reports that on the night of 17 November red and green clouds of colour were seen in the sky.

SCIENTISTS

Kent has been the birthplace of army and naval officers, writers, revolutionaries and artists, but some of its sons were scientists.

One of the best-known scientists of the Victorian period was Charles Darwin, who wrote *On the Origin of Species* at Downe House in the village of Downe, near Orpington, where he lived for the last forty years of his life.

The technological advancement of the navy was made possible by Sir Francis Pettit-Smith, who in 1836 took out a patent on a screw-propeller, which was bought by the navy and subsequently used instead of paddle propulsion.

Lastly, the Reverend Joseph Bancroft Reade, rector of Bishopsbourne, was a Fellow of the Royal Society and of the Royal Meteorological Society and paved the way for many future inventions. He was the first Englishman to photograph the moon and the first to illuminate slide specimens and use this technique to examine fossil organisms. His design for a telescope eyepiece won a medal at the Great Exhibition in 1851, and he designed a condenser called Reade's kettledrum, as well as a type of prism. He also took out an ink patent in 1846.

THE QUEEN'S JUBILEES

In 1887 the little village of Shalmsford joined in the celebrations of Queen Victoria's Golden Jubilee, when there was a fete on Chartham village green, with tea provided for the aged, the poor and children, along with sports and a chance to listen to the City Band. Everyone was granted a day's holiday and the day ended with fireworks.

The *Kentish Gazette* reports that Alfred Foreman gave a garden party for young people aged 14–25, providing a sit-down tea for fifty-five people. They were joined later in the evening by twenty-seven tenants who gave a rousing rendition of the National Anthem to accompany a firework display and then danced until gone 11 o'clock. This type of celebration was repeated across the county and villagers would also have been able to see some of the Golden Jubilee beacons which straddled the country.

In 1897 similar festivities were seen across Kent to celebrate the Diamond Jubilee. The residents enjoyed another fete on Chartham village green, which was decorated with Chinese lanterns and 200 flags. The children of Kent were presented with medals and brooches, which were commissioned locally, possibly via private funding, and the Diamond Jubilee beacons once again spanned the country as a sign of unity.

North Foreland Lighthouse, on the most easterly part of the Isle of Thanet

LITERARY CONNECTIONS

Although born in Portsmouth, Charles Dickens moved to Kent with his family when he was 4, and remained a happy resident, eventually buying Gad's Hill Place, near Rochester. The author had well-documented stays in Broadstairs and Folkestone as well as the Medway towns and his books reflect many aspects of Kent life, not least the hulks situated offshore at Cooling.

William Morris lived at the Red House in Upton near Bexleyheath, which was then in Kent, for little more than five years, but his personal touches have made it a distillation of his work and ethos. Visitors can see his hand in the design of almost every aspect of life there. He and his wife Jane were visited frequently by the friends who became famous as the Pre-Raphaelite Brotherhood.

Richard Barham took the pen name Thomas Ingoldsby and became a household name through his series *The Ingoldsby Legends* which appeared throughout the nineteenth century in magazines. It was he who first referred to the Romney Marsh as 'the fifth continent'.

LOSING PART OF KENT

The County of London was created by the Local Government Act in 1888 and the new county incorporated parts of north-west Kent, including Deptford, Greenwich, Woolwich and Lewisham. Ten years later, the county gained Penge, but this was only for a brief spell, and it was soon subsumed into the London Borough of Bromley. It is interesting to note that from the Norman Conquest until 1888 North Woolwich, situated on the northern banks of the River Thames, had been administered as part of Kent, and was variously known as North Woolwich, Woolwich in Essex or even Kent in Essex.

13

THE HOUSE OF SAXE-COBURG-GOTHA

≁ 1901–1917 ≀

On the death of Queen Victoria in 1901 the royal house took the name of her husband, Prince Albert of Saxe-Coburg-Gotha. King Edward VII reigned for only nine years until 1910. For his coronation in 1902, a large crown was cut into the chalk of a hillside near Wye, which is still visible today. Fifteen hundred fairy lights were used to illuminate it on that night, and it again blazed across the countryside in 1935 and 1977 for the Silver Jubilees of George V and Elizabeth II. The crown is also illuminated on Guy Fawkes' Night each year and has been recently refurbished.

Edward liked Kent, and Folkestone's Grand Metropole Hotel was a favourite destination as it was one of the places where he met his mistress, Alice Keppel. Mrs Keppel was a charismatic character, and although she was twenty-six years younger than he, she became a close confidante and adviser. Her warmth and discretion made her an able and effective mistress, bringing happiness to the king and at times acting as a liaison between him and his ministers.

THE AGE OF THE AIRCRAFT

In 1909 Louis Blériot flew across the English Channel from Calais to Dover, the first person to do so in a heavier-than-air plane. The plane was a very basic model and he had to be guided by smoke sent up from a French destroyer before making a crash landing in Northfall Meadow, behind Dover Castle. An aircraft-sized stone memorial was erected where he landed.

In the same year, the Short brothers opened the world's first aircraft factory on the Isle of Sheppey, which paved the way for the future of air travel and aerospace engineering. The Wright brothers had made history in 1903 when they flew the Wright Flyer in North Carolina, USA, and they granted a licence to Oswald, Horace and Eustace Short to build the Wright Flyer in the UK at Shellness. An Aero Club was set up, and members included Charles Rolls, who asked for a glider in which he could teach himself to fly (this became the Short-Wright Flyer), and J.T.C. Moore-Brabazon, who became the first man to fly a British-built aircraft. Moore-Brabazon, Charles Rolls and Frank McClean, who bought and tested several of their planes, set the pace for aircraft development and by 1910 the industry had outgrown the site, which was closed when operations were moved to Eastchurch. Before this happened, one last major achievement for the site was the design of the world's first swept-wing aircraft, which was built by the Short brothers, but created by J.W. Dunne. Further designs with more advanced features were built at the Eastchurch plant.

The Wright Flyer, built under licence on the Isle of Sheppey

In 1911 Frank McClean allowed the Admiralty to use some of his land to develop naval flying and in 1911 the Royal Naval Air Service, forerunner of the Royal Air Force, was born.

King George V came to the throne on the death of his father in 1910 and ruled for the next twenty-six years.

KENT COALFIELDS

The first Kent coalfield opened 1913 and was bringing up coal until 1989. Coal was first discovered in Kent by the Victorians in 1891, in the spoils of a failed attempt to dig a Channel Tunnel, and the Kent coal industry was born. Tilmanstone and Snowdown pits were opened in 1914 and Chislet in 1918. Betteshanger, near Deal, followed in 1924. The villages of Aylesham, Elvington and Heresden were built for the miners, each complete with shops and a community centre. Once local coal was found, it was inevitable that electricity generating stations would be built nearby and these were soon erected at Richborough and Dungeness.

In 1912 the East Kent Light Railway opened to serve the coal mines in the area. However, two wars intervened, it was not used as much as expected and in 1948 it closed as a commercial venture. In 1985, though, the East Kent Light Railway Society was formed, and the line still operates today, manned by volunteers who also run a small museum.

THE FIRST WORLD WAR

To cope with the demand for fighting men, a new regiment was formed in Kent, and at the end of August 1914 a notice appeared in the *Kentish Gazette*: 'A call to all men of Kent. Your country asks for soldiers, you the successors of the men of Kent who were never vanquished in all the centuries past, must respond to the call ... Every man who joins will earn honour for himself, the gratitude of his friends and the thanks of his country. A new battalion of the Buffs is being formed, join at once.' Within a week the Royal East Kent Regiment, as it was known, was almost 1,000-strong and the Royal West Kent Regiment had enlisted an equal number.

In December 1914, Kent experienced the first bomb attacks on civilian targets, as Zeppelin airships passed Kent on their way towards London and took the opportunity to bomb the ports of Folkestone and Dover as they went.

The port of Richborough was brought into service for the duration of the war, although it is all but invisible in the modern landscape. Vast numbers of men and horses and tons of materials were shipped to Flanders from the warehouses that once lined the forgotten wharf. Camps on either side of the River Stour were occupied by thousands of soldiers who were carried to France by specially constructed sea-going barges, along with munitions and rations for both horse and man. The secret base even had its own railway.

The Dover Patrol was formed in 1914 around a core of twelve destroyers. Along with submarines and minesweepers, these ships patrolled the Channel and the North Sea during the war. A stone column was erected in Dover as a memorial to the men who gave their lives while serving in the patrol during the First and Second World Wars. It is estimated that 2,000 men of the patrol died in these conflicts.

An airship at Kingsnorth

Thousands of men across Kent signed up and many gave their lives, but the tiny village of Knowlton in particular has much to be thankful for. Of the village's 39 residents, 12 signed up and left for battle, and somehow they all returned safely. A tall stone monument stands testament to the bravery of those men who were willing to give everything, while a more modern plaque, identifying Knowlton as one of the Thankful Villages where no lives were lost, acts as a reminder of the folly of war rather than of individual stories.

In 1915 the airship works at Kingsnorth was tasked with developing a Submarine Scout airship, whose purpose was to spot enemy submarines. After a successful first flight in March 1915, ships were put into production and by the end of the war 35 Coastal Class submarine scouts had been built on the site.

Gunpowder production increased during this period, and the Kent works at Cliffe and Faversham were amongst the largest. Despite stringent safety regulations, an explosion in 1916 at the Chart Works, Faversham, killed 106 men. It was in this year that British Summer Time was introduced to increase productivity.

The Royal Air Force was formed in 1918 by merging the Royal Naval Air Service and the Royal Flying Corps. During the war, private airstrips had been pressed into national service and tiny places such as Bekesbourne, Detling, Penshurst, Harrietsham, Jesson, Joyce Green, Marden and Yokes Court were developed as air bases, alongside the larger ones at Dover, Rochester, Manston, Lydd and Hawkinge.

After the war, 200 towns across the UK were gifted with a tank to thank them for contributions given during the war. The boys of our Kentish family were fascinated to see one roll past their home on the way to St George's

Square in Ashford that summer. The Mark 4 'female' tank is the only one of her type left in situ as most were scrapped during the Second World War for their metal content. The tank at Ashford was not reused as it housed the town's electricity transformer. It has become a listed building and acts as a war memorial to those who died.

Hundreds of other war memorials exist throughout the county, paying tribute to the thousands of men who lost their lives, but one of the most obvious is the large cross cut into the chalk on the hillside above Shoreham, and one of the most impressive is the Memorial Arch at the top of Remembrance Hill in Folkestone, which was unveiled in 2014 to mark the centenary of the outbreak of the war.

14

THE HOUSE OF
WINDSOR

⇥ 1917– ⇤

As the rumblings of the First World War began to
make themselves heard and pitted families against
each other, King George V changed his family name
from the German 'Saxe-Coburg-Gotha' to the English-
sounding 'Windsor'.

BETWEEN THE WARS

Once the First World War had ended, our Kentish family
were keen to get back to normal as soon as possible.
Rationing had been introduced in 1918 and continued
until 1920. However, they were pleased to see that airports such as Lympne were being returned to civilian
use, although of course many were requisitioned again in
the Second World War.

New building work started, holidays were once
again possible, and the number of visitors to towns like

Folkestone and Margate increased. This was an era of hope for the future.

CHARTWELL

Winston Spencer-Churchill acquired Chartwell in 1922. He used the house mainly as a weekend retreat when it was first built, before moving in permanently during the 1930s. The property is now in the ownership of the National Trust, so visitors can wander the garden or peep into Churchill's library or studio and see the Mary Cot playhouse he built for his youngest daughter.

ACOUSTIC MIRRORS

After the shock of the First World War, the government was mindful that another war might occur, and started to devise methods of warning and protecting the country. Modern technological advances in the 1920s saw the development of 'acoustic mirrors', which were installed around the coast of Britain to listen for incoming aircraft and thus warn of impending attack. The mirrors were said to be able to detect aircraft from 20 miles away. The site at Dungeness includes two concrete 'sound mirrors' and a 200ft curved concrete wall, all intended to funnel sound to strategically placed microphones which sent signals to the adjoining listening room. This is the only site in Britain where all three designs are situated in one place and they remained in place after the development of radar to be used in case of radar failure. By 1936, however, they were to all intents and purposes obsolete.

TIME TO PLAY

Originally at a terminus for London, Chatham and Dover Railway trains, the site at Dreamland was first opened in the 1860s under the name 'The Hall by the Sea' when it was a tea room and dance hall. The site was later extended to include a zoo (yes, there were elephants!) and pleasure gardens. The name Dreamland was used from the 1920s, when the famous rollercoaster-cum-scenic railway was constructed. Further fun park attractions were added, but the park's popularity dwindled and it closed in 2003. After several failed regeneration attempts, it is once again undergoing refurbishment.

The Romney, Hythe and Dymchurch Railway is a bit of an oddity and, although loved by children and enthusiasts, is sometimes tolerated like an eccentric relative rather than being celebrated as it should be. Over 13 miles are travelled by steam and diesel trains of one-third the full size, and it has become world famous and one of Kent's top tourist attractions.

The railway was built by two eccentric millionaires: Captain Howey and Count Louis Zborowski, owner of the famous Chitty Chitty Bang Bang car. The official opening took place in July 1927, with an inaugural train ride from Hythe to New Romney. The railway was, perhaps surprisingly, requisitioned by the War Department in the Second World War and it was used extensively during the building of PLUTO (Pipe Line Under The Ocean) which fuelled the Allied invasion force.

Our Kentish family were delighted in 1929 when Chatham Dockyard held its first Navy Day. The yard was opened so that the public could see how it worked and watch specially created displays. Navy Days were an annual event until 1982, when the Falklands War started, and the navy finally moved out of the base in 1984. The whole site has now been opened as a museum, including information on the RNLI, and it houses the largest collection of historic lifeboats in the UK.

The children of the Kentish family were thrilled when Maidstone Zoo opened in 1934, and were keen to visit whenever they could. They were particularly fond of the zoo's two elephants, Gert and Daisy, whose house can be found by the keen investigator in Cobtree Park. The zoo was the brainchild of Hugh Garrard Tyrwhitt-Drake, twelve times Mayor of Maidstone and also High Sheriff of Kent. Sadly, the Second World War intervened and the zoo closed in 1959.

In 1935 the king celebrated his Silver Jubilee, an occasion of great public rejoicing. The street parties which had been so popular after the First World War were revived, allowing communities to celebrate together.

After the death of George V, the Lord Mayor of London proposed that a fitting memorial would be the establishment of a series of playing fields throughout the country as a permanent reminder of the king. Accordingly, a committee was set up and 471 fields were established in towns across the UK, with fields in Kent at places such as Westerham, Sittingbourne, Queenborough, Maidstone, Canterbury, Cranbrook and Faversham plus fields in smaller towns and villages such as Temple Ewell and Loose.

King George VI came to the throne after the death of his father in 1936 and was crowned in 1937. The coronation robes were made from silk grown at the silkworm farm at Lullingstone Castle, as was the satin gown of the Queen Mother. Later the same silkworms produced silk for the wedding dress of Princess Elizabeth.

THE KITCHENER CAMP FOR REFUGEES

As Hitler continued his persecution of the German Jews, many fled to England. The former army camp near Sandwich was adapted by the Council of German Jewry to house Jewish men from Germany, Czechoslovakia and Austria who had been released from concentration camps on the proviso that they would leave Germany immediately. Almost 5,000 men arrived and were housed and cared for. Later, many were able to arrange for their wives and children to join them and the camp developed into a self-contained village, trading with each other and shopping in the village of Sandwich when they needed to. At the end of the war, fewer than 1,000 remained and they were relocated further from the coast.

THE SECOND WORLD WAR

When war was declared on 1 September 1939, Kent prepared for invasion. Steel scaffolding and barbed-wire fences were put up along the beaches, guns, anti-tank ditches, anti-aircraft batteries and pillboxes were built, anti-tank traps and minefields were installed and leaflets were printed in their thousands. Our Kentish family and their neighbours were still reeling from the previous war and hoped it would all be over much faster this time. Dover in particular was targeted by the enemy, and as it is only 22 miles from Calais it was bombed by huge guns shooting across the Channel.

During the first months of the war, children and families were evacuated into Kent, and our Kentish family were pleased to give rooms to a family from London, who loved their life in the country. As the months slipped by, however, it became clear that Kent was no longer a safe place to be and children were advised to move in with distant relatives if they could. Those who could not were relocated as evacuees. One Sunday in June almost 3,000 children were moved from Dover to Monmouthshire in Wales to escape the county that became known as 'bomb alley'.

One of the places where people could shelter during an air raid was in the tunnels previously dug for chalk extraction at Margate. They could also use the tunnels at Ramsgate that were built during the 1940s and could shelter over 1,000 people. Parts of these tunnels are open to the public, and tours can be booked. People like our Kentish family who had enough room in their back garden built an Anderson Shelter and covered it with earth so the land could be used for short-rooted vegetables. They dug up the back lawn to plant more vegetables and kept chickens at the end of the garden. When rationing began, a family's quota of eggs could be converted into an allowance of chicken feed.

As war took hold of the county, civilian airports were once more taken into military hands and the two RAF bases of Biggin Hill and Manston became central to manoeuvres.

THE DUNKIRK EVACUATION

In the summer of 1940 a pincer movement by the German army cut off over 300,000 Allied troops on the coast near Dunkirk, France, and on 27 May Operation Dynamo was put into effect, overseen by officers stationed in the tunnels underneath Dover Castle. The Ministry of Shipping asked for any privately owned boats with a shallow draft to join their own ships in the rescue attempt. Around 700 boats, barges, yachts, lifeboats and ships all met at Sheerness where they were fuelled and sent to Ramsgate Harbour, where they were allocated navy personnel, in some cases supported by the boats' own crew. As these boats were able to get in close to the French shoreline, many having a draft of as little as 2ft, their task was to ferry soldiers to the larger vessels, although many did carry men all the way back to England. The evacuation lasted nine days, during which time 338,000 troops were rescued; 80,000 soldiers landed at Ramsgate and over 200,000 made it to Dover, to be ferried onwards by train. The soldiers and rescuers were offered food prepared by the Women's Institute, whose volunteers worked in shifts to provide constant refreshment.

Several ships that had been built in Kent joined the evacuation, and Thames barges were particularly useful due to their extremely shallow draft. The fact that they did not have engines made them useful for carrying munitions and many had already been taken under military control. The paddle steamer *Medway Queen* had been commissioned in 1939 and made seven runs during the evacuation, rescuing 7,000 men and earning herself the nickname 'Heroine of Dunkirk'.

The half-dozen Thames barges were accompanied by two other extraordinary craft: the *Lady Haig*, which was a clinker-built open boat known as a 'hoveller', and *Tamzine*, which was also an open fishing boat.

Following the rescue, Churchill was quick to point out that Operation Dynamo had been a retreat and should not be seen as a victory, and yet it gave a huge boost to public morale and the whole country was proud of the brave men who took part.

THE BATTLE OF BRITAIN

The children of our Kentish family felt terrified and delighted in equal measure in the summer of 1940 when they watched the Battle of Britain unfold overhead. German aircraft began by attacking RAF airfields at various locations and then targeted other inland airfields and aircraft factories. On 15 September, things came to a head and a concerted effort led to a dog-fight in the skies above Kent; time after time, waves of British Spitfires met waves of German aircraft. At the end of the battle, after three and a half months of fighting, Britain had lost twenty-five aircraft compared to Germany's ninety-seven and had won the day. The Spitfire and Hurricane Memorial Museum RAF Manston records the events of the period and the bravery of the men who took part, while the visitor centre at the Battle of Britain memorial at Hawkinge, near Folkestone, which was unveiled by Her Majesty the Queen Mother in July 1993, also houses a collection of artefacts and memorabilia.

In 1940 a group of Indian soldiers arrived in England, and a statue in Gravesend of fighter pilot Squadron Leader Mahinder Singh Pujji has been erected to represent service personnel from across the world who have fought for Britain in conflicts since 1914.

There were two main prisoner-of-war camps in Kent during the Second World War, one at Shorncliffe and one at Somerhill, although there were satellite camps at Folkestone, Somerhill, Stanhope, Woodchurch, Chatham, Swanscombe, Ravensbourne, Chislehurst, Mereworth, Brissenden, Tonbridge, Wouldham and Dover.

The anti-aircraft defence system at West Malling is one of the few places where you can see a Bofors light anti-aircraft gun tower. Erected in 1940 and working with a

Pickett-Hamilton fort and a Type 24 pillbox, these structures were built to defend West Malling airfield.

The Kent Women's Land Army Museum at Little Farthingloe Farm, Dover, gives a fascinating insight into the role of women in the Kent countryside during the war. All able-bodied men had been drafted, but the land still needed to be worked, not only to maintain, but also to increase production to feed the nation, making up for the shortfall caused by the German blockade on supply ships. One of the Land Army bases was at Ivychurch, where women lived in communal dormitories. They were issued with a bike and a uniform and worked in the fields alongside those men left behind, dodging bombs as they worked.

By 1941, the national workforce was so depleted that all women aged 18–60 had to register as available for work and a feminist milestone was reached. The men who were not in the military had already signed up to the Civil Defence Service and were engaged in first-aid work, the fire watcher service, gas decontamination, as wardens or in observation or welfare units. Women not in full-time employment joined the Women's Voluntary Service. The Local Defence Volunteers (LDVs) were formed in 1940, and within the first twenty-four hours the country had a force of 250,000 17–65-year-olds wanting to take a role in defending their country. The role of the LDVs, in the case of invasion, was to try to slow down the advance of the enemy, even by only a few hours, in order to give the regular forces time to regroup. The men of the Kentish family were used to using firearms and were members of the local gun club, so they were particularly welcome. The force is sometimes derided as being a 'Dad's Army', but by the end of the war over 1,000 men had given their lives in service.

The so-called Baedecker raids started in April 1942, and Canterbury was badly damaged. The raids were so named after Baron Braun von Stumm reportedly said, 'We shall go out and bomb every building in Britain marked with three stars in the *Baedeker Guide*.' Outside of Canterbury, where Sturry was badly affected, Deal suffered notable casualties and thirty people died.

Maunsell sea forts were installed off the Kent coast in 1942 to counteract attacks from the Luftwaffe, who were using the Thames as a navigation aid on their way to bomb London, safe in the knowledge that no anti-aircraft guns could reach them. The three sets of forts, Shivering Sands, Red Sands and Nore, were built at Red Lion Wharf in Northfleet and floated down the river to be used as platforms for anti-aircraft guns. Each fort had seven towers, linked by walkways, high above the river surface. There were initially 165 men in each tower, which was increased to 265 in 1944 to counter the V1 flying bomb threat.

The forts were briefly used as a home for pirate radio stations in 1964–5, but have since been abandoned. On a clear day, they can be seen from Whitstable and Herne Bay, and boat trips allow a closer look, but the forts themselves are no longer accessible due to their poor condition.

Also in 1942, Richborough Camp, so useful during the First World War, became a post of the Marines, and was re-named HMS Robertson. Part of the Mulberry Harbour which was towed to the Normandy coast for the D-Day attack was built there by the Royal Engineers.

The Women's Institute (WI) had been formed in 1915 to revitalise rural communities and encourage women to become more involved in the production of food during the First World War. As you might guess, Kent has West Kent and East Kent branches, both of which

The Maunsell sea forts in the Thames Estuary

started towards the end of the First World War. Branches throughout the county acted as collection points for supplies for the troops, and Barham WI was honoured for its contribution to the war effort when Eleanor Roosevelt visited in 1942.

As well as enemy ordnance, Kent saw many explosions of our own bombs when Barnes Wallis tested his bouncing bomb off the coast at Reculver. After testing, it was used by the 617 squadron in May 1943 to critically damage three dams in the German Ruhr valley. Both the Upkeep and Highball weapons were developed at RAF Manston and it was here that the crews of the Lancaster bombers assembled under Squadron Leader Guy Gibson. A bronze statue to the inventor was erected on Herne Bay seafront in 2008.

In 1944 Kent was washed with a wave of V1 and V2 bombs – the infamous 'doodlebugs', which rained down on the country for a year. It was in the same year that the SS *Richard Montgomery* sank off the coast of Kent, on the Nore sandbank. She had been carrying munitions, and about 1,400 tonnes of explosives remain on board, presenting a hazard to shipping and those who live within a 10-mile radius, the expected extent of the blast range should it explode. Her masts remain visible at low tide, and even after all this time, opinion is divided on whether to leave her or move her.

The Kentish family were happy for the army to use their land during Operation Fortitude, which was a sleight-of-hand manoeuvre intended to distract the Germans while the D-Day landings were prepared and carried out, and lead them to think that the raid would take place in the Pas-de-Calais. A vast dummy army was assembled in the county, roads and bridges were built, army manoeuvres held and dummy landing craft, aircraft, tanks and military vehicles all created. The troops even mounted a mock invasion, leaving from Dover on 5 June accompanied by balloons, reflectors and smoke generators to give the impression of a full convoy of ships. This operation was a key part of the success of the D-Day landings.

As the first bomb of the war to fall in England had fallen on Kent (Dover), so the last bomb to fall in Britain also landed on Kent (Orpington) in 1945. Many villages had suffered extensive damage, and the guide to St Peter and St Paul, Farningham, tells us that during the course of the war the village had experienced an incredible 143 high-explosive bombs, twelve incendiary attacks, six flying bombs, one long-range rocket plus other assorted missiles.

POST-WAR EXPANSION

With the threats and uncertainty of the war firmly behind them, the people of Kent could look forward to building a solid future for themselves and their families. Life gradually returned to normal, although rationing on some items stayed in place until 1954. Our Kentish family were lucky to live on a farm and have access to wild food from the countryside around them. Their house had remained undamaged throughout the war, and they shook their heads as they saw the amount of new housing springing up around them.

One thing they did approve of was the creation in 1946 of the Bewl Water reservoir. It was followed in 1968 by the Bough Beech reservoir near Sevenoaks.

By 1949, things were looking up and Peter Adolph from Langton Green had plenty of time to spare when he left the RAF. He used his time to finalise plans for a game of table football he named *Subbuteo*, which he later sold to Waddingtons for £250,000. However, Kent remained home to *Subbuteo* until the early 1980s when manufacturing moved to Leeds.

On the evening of 31 January 1953, Kent was hit by a 6m-high tidal surge, which swept down the eastern coast of the UK. Only one person in north Kent, a sluice keeper at Belvedere, died. Some 600 acres of apple, pear and cherry trees were destroyed, glasshouses were wrecked and thousands of livestock were lost, and for the first time in 500 years it was possible to see the Wantsum flow between Thanet and the Kent mainland. Gasworks, power stations and factories suffered immense damage and the consequences to both arable and dairy farms were immediate and far-reaching. It has been described as the worst national peacetime disaster to hit the UK.

Despite this, the people of Kent rallied and joined in whole-heartedly with the coronation celebrations in June of that year.

One of the major employers in east Kent was the American company Pfizer, which opened a site in Folkestone in the mid-1950s and then moved to Sandwich, where it expanded its operations until the workforce out-numbered the residents of the small town. Despite local irritations about parking and housing prices, Pfizer did bring money into the area and people were sad to see it leave in 2012, finding it hilarious that the site was used in 2013 as the location for the Brad Pitt zombie film *World War Z*. Chatham Dockyard is the most-filmed historic location in Kent and has been used for *Children of Men*, *Les Miserables*, *Sherlock Holmes*, *The Crown* and *The Mummy*. The dockyard was also used in both *Downton Abbey* and *Call the Midwife*, which were made for TV. Knole Park was the setting for some scenes of *Pirates of the Caribbean: On Stranger Tides* and *The Other Boleyn Girl*. Dover Castle and Penshurst Place are also well used by the film industry, as well as the small village of Cliffe on the Hoo Peninsula, which was used by Stanley Kubrik as the setting for *Full Metal Jacket*.

On a more serious note, an underground bunker was built in Gravesend in 1954. It was a command post to be used by Gravesend's rescue and emergency services in the event of a nuclear attack.

POWERFUL STATIONS

Kent has a long history of heavy industry on the north Kent coast – where the acid heathland soil is unsuitable for agriculture – from ironworking to cement works, quarrying and papermaking, although as the twentieth century progressed, improvements in technology made some of the products redundant and others more easily and cheaply produced elsewhere in the world. Slowly the industrial landscape of the Medway area began to change and it became a major employer in the area.

A BP oil refinery opened in 1954 but closed 1984 when it was replaced by a Thamesport container terminal and later a BP liquid natural gas (LNG) berth for tankers. The power station on the Isle of Grain is owned by E.ON and uses natural gas, sending a by-product of heat to the nearby LNG station.

In southern Kent, the country's first atomic power station was opened at Dungeness in 1964, which was joined by Dungeness B in 1983. Dungeness A was decommissioned in 2012, but Dungeness B is still working and has a visitor centre where guests can learn more about the processes associated with a nuclear power station.

In the east, the coal-fired power station at Richborough opened in 1962 using coal from local coal fields, but was converted to oil in 1971. The demolition of the site started in 2000, and was completed in 2012 when the enormous cooling towers were blown up in front of a crowd of hundreds of local spectators.

OVER THE SEA

Kent is surrounded on three sides by water: the Thames to the north, the North Sea to the east and the English Channel to the south. Small wonder, then, that the county's history is inextricably linked with water as the sea is used for employment and leisure. Crossing the rivers, inlets and marshy ground has always been a challenge, but ingenuity has triumphed and Kent has a strong history of fords and ferries, bridges and tunnels used to navigate around and over the water.

Deal's pier was opened in November 1957 by HRH the Duke of Edinburgh and is the only remaining complete leisure pier in Kent. The current pier is its third incarnation, which has suffered over the years from weather and ship damage. The remains of Herne Bay Pier are visible from the shore, but it was closed in 1968 for reasons of safety. Looking at it today, it is hard to imagine its previous glory as the second longest pier in Britain, just falling short of the world-record-holding Southend Pier. It was badly damaged in storms, as was Margate's pleasure pier, which has now been demolished. Ramsgate and Broadstairs each have a pier, and Dover and Folkestone can boast two piers each.

The Kingsferry Bridge from the mainland to Sheppey was opened in 1959, and replaced by the Sheppey Crossing Bridge in 2006.

In 1962, Kent lost some of its towns as Greater London Council absorbed Orpington, Penge, Beckenham, Bromley, Bexley, Erith, Crayford, Chislehurst and Sidcup, and more were taken in 1965.

THE GREAT STORM

The Great Storm of 1987 was the worst storm in the area since 1703, sweeping across the county, ripping trees from the ground and tearing tiles from roofs. Caravans were upturned, boats thrown onto land, and outbuildings knocked sideways like firewood. Sevenoaks lost six of the trees that gave the town its name, and these were replanted, along with several others which will mature and be available should another disaster occur.

THE *HERALD OF FREE ENTERPRISE*

Dover is the busiest passenger port in the world and one of its main functions is as a ferry port between the UK and the continent. In April 1987, the ferry *Herald of Free Enterprise* capsized soon after leaving Zeebrugge, Belgium, on its way to Dover with a loss of 193 lives. This shocked the local community and the nation alike as it was the largest loss of life since the war. One of the memorials is a stained-glass window in St Mary's Church, Dover.

LITERARY CONNECTIONS

W. Somerset Maugham wrote *Of Human Bondage* in Whitstable, but was apparently not fond of the town, which he associated with an unhappy childhood. Sir Arthur Conan Doyle also visited regularly, although he did not live in Kent, and he set six of his stories in Kent towns and villages. It was the coming of the railway which allowed him to visit freely, and he was much taken with the beauty of the countryside through which he travelled and which features in the stories.

Siegfried Sassoon was born in Matfield in west Kent and many of his books refer to his life as a privileged young man, which was brought to an end when he was called up at the age of 27. He never returned to Kent, but instead settled in Wiltshire. Nevertheless, his earlier works present a view of a particular side of Kentish life.

Ian Fleming was also a visitor and wrote *You Only Live Twice* while staying at The Duck Inn at Pett Bottom. Several sources note that the No. 7 bus passes The Duck on its way from Dover to London; perhaps this was the inspiration for James Bond's number, 007. Another visitor was John Buchan, who wrote *The Thirty-Nine Steps* at Broadstairs, having stayed there many times with his family and used an old oak staircase that ran from his lodgings down to a private beach.

Some favourite children's characters are also connected with Kent. Rupert the Bear was written and illustrated by Mary Tourtel, who invented the character in 1920, and Bagpuss and the Clangers are the creations of Peter Firmin, who lived near Canterbury.

MOTORSPORT

Kent has had a long association with motor vehicles; in 1894 the first motor show was held near Tunbridge Wells. It was expected to be a small affair, held one Tuesday afternoon in October, with the expectation of a few hundred visitors. As it turned out, thousands arrived and a new phenomenon was born.

Lydden Hill is a motor racing venue offering a variety of events on two, three and four wheels, and our Kentish family often take the opportunity to visit for a thrilling day out. The mixed-surface circuit, made up of both firm and loose surfaces, was the birthplace of rallycross back in 1967 and it is now the venue for national and international events including the FIA World Rallycross, the BHP Show, the Classic Festival, Vintage Motorcyle Racing, the BTRC Truck Festival, the British Drift Championship, British Supermoto and the MSA British Rallycross.

The Brands Hatch motor racing circuit in West Kingsdown started out as a grass-track motorcycle circuit on farmland, but has since developed into a centre for motor sport and has hosted twelve runnings of the

British Grand Prix. It continues to host many British and international racing events.

RELIGIOUS TOLERANCE

Our Kentish family have been Anglican since the Reformation, with Canterbury Cathedral as the centre of their religion, but they have many friends who are Methodists, Jehovah's Witnesses, Jews, Baptists or Sikhs, all of whom have significant centres in Kent.

The Sikh temple or Gurdwara in Gravesend is one of the largest Sikh places of worship outside India; the marble carvings and brightly painted dome draw Sikh and non-Sikh visitors alike. Many of the Sikhs in the area immigrated in the late 1950s, and the temple is known for the colourful Sikh New Year celebrations each April.

The family's Jewish friends have major synagogues in Margate, Ramsgate and Chatham, and strong communities in other areas. The Jehovah's Witness community is also strong, with a Kingdom Hall in almost every large town in the county.

AN ACT OF TERRORISM

The whole of east Kent was rocked when a bomb exploded at the barracks of the Royal Marine School of Music in Deal in September 1989; eleven young men lost their lives and many more were injured. It being a music school, the men had played an active role in the local community, attending many high-profile events, and the Deal Memorial Bandstand was erected in 1993, paid for by local contributions. Despite the fact that the school has been moved to Portsmouth, the members travel to Deal each year to play a concert in memory of those lost. No one has ever been convicted of the attack, but it was reportedly the work of the Irish Republican Army (IRA), which planted the bomb the night before and detonated it by remote control.

CROSSING THE RIVER THAMES

The first Dartford Tunnel opened in 1963, giving travellers the opportunity to cross the Thames into Essex without going into London. The tunnel was a popular choice and in 1976 a second tunnel was opened. In 1991 the Queen Elizabeth II Bridge was opened to take southbound traffic, allowing both tunnels to be used as a northbound route. Around 50 million people use the QEII Bridge each year, up by 20 million since it was opened. In November 2014 the tollbooths were removed and payment for crossing has to be made online, speeding up crossing times.

The Tilbury to Gravesend ferry is a foot passenger service, although pedal bicycles can also be taken on board. The ferry runs up to twice an hour and the crossing takes ten minutes, depending on river traffic.

CROSSING THE ENGLISH CHANNEL

Even though Britain became separated from mainland Europe by the English Channel, we have maintained trading links, from the time of the Bronze Age boat, through the ages of smuggling and piracy to the present day. Kings and queens have passed through our ports, in and out of the country, on official visits and on secret missions.

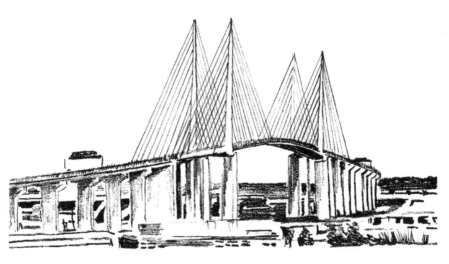

The Queen Elizabeth II Bridge at Dartford

The first crossing by hot air balloon took place in 1785, by Jean-Pierre Blanchard and his American co-pilot John Jeffries. They had first tried an ascent with a dog, a sheep and a cockerel and decided it was probably safe for a human being to ascend to the required altitude before going up themselves.

Once only the prerogative of the richest people, travelling for pleasure became much more accessible once the railways had arrived and were able to transport passengers directly to the point of departure. From 1842, the South East Railway Company started a service between London and Folkestone, enabling travellers to board the steamer for Boulogne. Ferries run regularly from Dover, Folkestone and Ramsgate, although the hovercraft service from Folkestone and the service from Sheerness to

Flushing are no longer in operation. The port of Dover was expanded in 1952 to take car ferries and it became a cruise terminal in 1996, from where passengers could embark on tours worldwide. There was also a catamaran service from Folkestone that operated for eight years from 1992 to 2000.

The first person to swim the Channel was Captain Webb, who did so in 1875. Since then about 4,000 swims have been made, with almost all the swimmers being in their mid-thirties. Male swimmers slightly outnumber the female. An average swim takes over thirteen hours and each swimmer is accompanied by a team of supporters and medical staff.

In June 1910, Charles Rolls, of Rolls-Royce fame, was the first man to fly from England to France and back again, a journey that took ninety-five minutes. Sadly, he took another record the next month when he became the first Briton to be killed in an aeronautical accident involving a powered aircraft.

THE CHANNEL TUNNEL

The idea of a tunnel under the Channel was first put forward by Frenchman Albert Mathieu in 1802, who suggested that France and England were linked by a road tunnel. He envisioned ventilation chimneys which would rise above the level of the water and an island mid-point to rest the horses. The tunnel would have been lit by oil-lamp.

It was not until the late twentieth century that plans were finalised, although there had been some unsuccessful attempts by Victorian entrepreneurs. Tunnelling began at Cheriton in 1988 and the tunnel finally met the French, who were digging from their side, in 1990, becoming the longest undersea tunnel in the world. Spoil from the tunnel was built up under the Lower Shakespeare Cliff near Dover and the new land has become a thriving nature conservation area, Samphire Hoe. The tunnel (actually a grouping of three tunnels) was formally opened in 1997 and carries 50,000 passengers each day.

Ashford station was demolished and reimagined in 1994 as Ashford International Station, for the purpose of servicing traffic to the tunnel, but in 2007 Ebbsfleet International was made the principal stop between Ashford and the continent.

High Speed 1, a fast train through the tunnel and across the county, was introduced in November 2007 starting at London St Pancras.

SPORT

Our Kentish family like to play in and watch local sports teams, from Bat and Trap at the local pub on a summer's evening to the occasional visit to Priestfield Stadium to watch Gillingham FC, which is Kent's only league football team.

Canterbury is the home of both the Kent County Cricket Club, founded in 1890, and the Kent Women's Cricket Team, which was formed in 1997. The town is also home to the Canterbury Hockey Club and the Holcombe Hockey Club, which play at international level.

The county has two National League netball clubs, both based in north-west Kent, and owns several top-class sporting facilities. Folkestone Sports Centre has a dry ski slope, and the Royal St George's Golf Course is used in rotation for the British Open Golf Tournament.

The Julie Rose Stadium is regarded as one of the finest athletics facilities in the country.

One game that is no longer played is the fast and furious game of Goal Running, which died out in the 1940s, and is peculiar to Kent. Teams of ten members played barefoot on whichever village green or playing field was available, under the guidance of a referee in a game much like the popular schoolyard sport of tag. The attendance at one match in 1950 was over 3,000, but it was a localised speciality and, as tastes widened, spectators preferred to watch nationally approved games such as football.

RESTRUCTURING THE MEDWAY TOWNS

Another administrative reshuffle in 1998 took the Medway towns of Gillingham, Chatham and Rochester, along with their surrounding villages, out of the county of Kent, giving them their own status as the Medway Unitary Authority. Due to an administrative error during the application process, Rochester lost its 'city' status, and despite several re-applications, this has never been reinstated.

BLUEWATER SHOPPING CENTRE

Building started in 1996 on the shopping centre that has become England's largest shopping mall, complete with 50 acres of parks, a young driver centre and four cinema screens. The centre at Greenhithe was built on the site of a disused quarry and opened in 1999, after which it quickly won a bevy of awards.

EDUCATION

Although much of Britain adopted a comprehensive education system in the 1970s, Kent County Council and Medway Unitary Authority decided to provide selective education for the young people of Kent. Students can sit the 'Kent Test' at the end of Year 6 and if they pass, can choose to attend one of the thirty-three grammar schools in Kent and Medway. If not, they attend a secondary modern school.

Kent has four universities: Canterbury Christ Church University, the University of Kent, the University of Greenwich (a London University with sites at Woolwich, Eltham, London and Medway) and the University for the Creative Arts, which has three of its five campuses in the county. The University of Kent and Canterbury Christ Church University enrol 20,000 students each year.

15

MODERN TIMES

⚜ 2000 – ⚜

The House of Windsor continues, as Queen Elizabeth II becomes the longest-serving regent in our history. The rise in the population of England does not abate, and the number of residents stands at over 55 million.

Kent joined in wholeheartedly with the nation's celebrations of the new millennium, with St Margaret's Bay even claiming to be the most westerly point of the UK, and therefore the first place for the dawn of the new millennium to break. Some of the permanent reminders of the celebrations are the clock in Tunbridge Wells town centre, the 20-acre Biddenden Millennium Fields and the KM Millennium Bridge at Whatman Park in Maidstone, among others.

THE GURKHAS

Gurkha soldiers from Nepal have fought alongside the British army for 200 years, with their main base traditionally in the British territory of Hong Kong. In 2001, when

Hong Kong reverted to Chinese control, the Royal Gurkha Rifles came to Britain, with the largest group living and working in Folkestone. The Gurkhas and their families are popular members of the local community, sharing their Nepalese customs with schools, WIs etc. Those Gurkhas who retired after 1997 were given the right to remain in the UK and pension rights equal to other members of the armed services. Following a high-profile campaign by celebrity Joanna Lumley, Gurkhas who retired before this date have now been granted the same privileges.

MANSTON AIRPORT CLOSES

Our Kentish family had fallen into the habit of taking their holidays abroad, and liked to travel by ferry from Dover or Folkestone or to fly to the Netherlands from Manston International Airport. However, in May 2014 Manston airport was finally closed, after much local debate and protestation, thus ending a 100-year history of the site, including the development of Barnes Wallis' bouncing bomb and a leading role in the Battle of Britain. The airport was one of the few places in the country with a runway long enough to accept big planes like Concorde, and once ran short pleasure flights on the iconic airplane. It will be sadly missed.

DAILY LIFE

Daily life for the Kentish family is much the same as it has been for the preceding 100 years. They are lucky enough to own the land they live on and to make a sustainable living from the farm. They have had to diversify as the price of some of their staple crops has dropped dramatically, and they have changed the way they use the land to grow a selection of herbs as well as flowers for the perfume trade. They are moving towards organic production methods in order to increase profits.

The village in which they live has seen a decline, and they have lost most of their shops and their Post Office. Compared to the thriving community of 100 years ago, the area is almost unrecognisable. The advent of the high-speed train, while a good business tool to get produce to market in the early morning, has brought with it a generation of commuters who live in the village but are rarely at home. The family usually shop online or in the local big supermarket, and they are waiting for the introduction of high-speed broadband, ruing the fact that the tiny villages which need it most are the last to get it. Their children have moved away as they can no longer afford to live in the village, but happily they live within easy travelling distance.

ANIMAL WELFARE

Kent has always been known for its agriculture and animal husbandry and these skills have translated into expertise in rearing and caring for wild or unwanted animals. Kent has sanctuaries for native birds of prey, foals, cats, dogs, birds and hedgehogs, as well as foundations like Port Lympne, Howletts Wild Animal Park, Wingham Wildlife Park and The Big Cat Sanctuary which cater for more exotic species.

John Aspinall, who made his money running casinos, set up both Howletts and Port Lympne, more as sanctuaries than zoos, and instigated hugely successful breeding programmes for endangered animals. Port Lympne offers a safari experience with over 700 animals on show, while keepers at Howletts have bred over fifty gorillas, along with hundreds of tigers, including the first Siberian tiger born in Britain, the first snow leopard to be born in captivity, the first honey badger to be bred in a zoo and the first Przewalski's horses to be bred for thirty years. The park is home to the largest herd of breeding African elephants in the UK – somewhat of a Kent speciality, you might say!

AONB

The Kent Downs, always loved by local people, are now designated and protected as an Area of Outstanding Natural Beauty (AONB), much of which falls in the county of Kent. The range, which follows the chalk and greensand ridge once walked by Neolithic travellers, is known for its chalk scrub, wooded areas and heathlands, and its surprising variety of wildlife. Included within the area are traditional Kentish orchards and hop gardens, the Pilgrims' Way and countless historical parks and villages. Visitors can take advantage of the area by walking the North Downs Way National Trail.

The High Weald, part of which also falls within Kent, is another AONB, famed for its woodlands and historical villages, and is considered to be one of the best surviving medieval landscapes in northern Europe.

NATIONAL NATURE RESERVES AND SSSI

With its diverse landscapes, Kent is lucky enough to have nature reserves which reflect a range of habitats. There are National Nature Reserves at Stodmarsh,

Swanscombe Skull Site, Blean Woods, Elmley, Ham Street Woods, Lydden Temple Ewell, Sandwich and Pegwell Bay, The Swale, Wye and High Halstow.

Dungeness has been designated as a National Nature Reserve (NNR), Special Protection Area (SPA) and Special Area of Conservation (SAC). It is home to 600 species of plants, which is a third of all plants found in the UK. The area is unique, comprising what at first glance seems to be a desolate landscape with wooden houses, power stations, lighthouses and expansive gravel pits, yet it possesses a rich and diverse wildlife in one of the largest shingle landscapes in the world. This is great for wildlife, but not so good for the people who live and work in the area. Once upon a time, residents and visitors were forced to wear 'backstays' (pronounced 'baxters') which were pieces of wood strapped to their boots so they could walk any distance over the shingle.

There are currently 98 Sites of Special Scientific Interest (SSSIs) in Kent, 21 noted for their geological interest, 67 for their biological interest and 10 for both.

The world's biggest wind farm opened in 2010 at Foreness Point, near Kinsgate on the Isle of Thanet, and the Kentish Flats wind farm off Whitstable has thirty turbines. It has been possible for these to be erected because of the high sandbanks off the coast of Kent – the very things which made it unsuitable for ships wanting to pull into port and bring prosperity to the region are now helping that to happen.

REGENERATION

Areas of Thanet, Dover, Ashford, Swale, Gravesham, Dartford and Shepway have been recorded as the poorest in the county, and fall within the top ten most deprived areas in the UK as a whole. Thanet in particular has seen a decline in town centre vibrancy over the years, with even the tourist trade becoming less frequent. Margate has had recent investment in the Old Quarter which has become a centre for artists and craftspeople, and it was chosen for the site of the Turner Contemporary Gallery, which brings in tourists from around the world. Folkestone, too, has seen an influx of artists, and proudly declares that 'Folkestone is an Art School'.

BREXIT

Britain joined the European Economic Community (EEC) in 1973, and in the national referendum of 1975 as to whether we should remain in it, the Kentish family voted to stay, along with the three-quarters of the county who voted the same.

The 2011 National Census data show us that 86 per cent of the population of the UK were born in England, Ireland, Scotland or Wales, 4 per cent were born in the European Union (EU) and just under 10 per cent were born in non-EU countries. Kent has benefited from a regular influx of refugees and migrant workers, bringing with them new skills and practices. However, immigration was one of the main issues that prompted the 2016 referendum on whether or not the UK should remain part of the European Union. The people of Kent voted overwhelmingly to leave, with Tunbridge Wells being the only district to vote 'remain'. Gravesham registered the biggest difference with over 65 per cent of the voters choosing the 'leave' option.

CONCLUSION

The history of the county of Kent has been long and varied. From the first footstep of man on virgin soil, through the ingenious use of ironstone, clay, coal and woodland to promote the growth of the nation, to the current emphasis on wildlife and landscape conservation, Kent has seen it all. Three-quarters of the county is still used as agricultural land, but we also give a home to more listed buildings than anywhere in the country outside of London, and welcome 60 million visitors a year to learn about our history, enjoy our present and speculate upon our future.

Whether you feel like a Kentish man or a man of Kent, you can be proud of many things. We are the Garden of England, England's frontline county, the birthplace of the British aviation industry and the first place to embrace Christianity.

Rejoice!

INDEX